Retrospect
The Story of an Analysis

EMMA THRAIL

Retrospect
The Story of an Analysis

EMMA THRAIL

QUARTET BOOKS

First published by Quartet Books Limited 1994
A member of the Namara Group
27 Goodge Street
London W1P 1FD

A catalogue record for this title is available from the British Library

ISBN 0 7043 7081 6
Phototypeset by Intype, London
Printed and bound in Great Britain by WBC Bookbinders, Mid Glamorgan.

for Ann Penny

'Life is fiction. Art is autobiography'

Peter Ackroyd

ACKNOWLEDGEMENTS

The author is grateful to Faber & Faber for permission to quote from the poems of Theodore Roethke, W. H. Auden and Michael Roberts and to Jonathan Cape Ltd. for Robert Frost.

This is the story of an ordinary life. So ordinary that to tell it in detail is hardly necessary. I can sum it up in a couple of sentences. It is about a girl with the correct number of parents: good parents, who lived good lives and long. A girl who did well at school and was popular, went to university, flirted briefly with a career, married and had the usual number of children, and settled down with the best of intentions to be a good wife and mother, while continuing, of course, to be a good daughter. She had no outstanding talents, no outstanding virtues; no outstanding vices either, except what she called inertia and her husband, mental laziness. From her schooldays on all were agreed that with a little effort she could do better. What could be more ordinary? What could be more unexceptional? Many would envy her. She was lucky her friends told her, she told herself. No tragedy. No insurmountable handicap. Yet at the age of forty she found life had no meaning for her and she was forced to admit (at the bottom of the pit where there is no point in telling anything but the truth) that it never had had. She had borrowed meaning from other people: their lives, their enthusiasms, their energies; imitating, emulating, hoping some of it would rub off on her, and she would be real in the end. Real in a real world, a world that up to now she had not felt she belonged in or had any right to inhabit.

(Inside is not ordinary. Inside is a different story: of 'Greater love hath no man . . .'; of 'our martyred dead' spilling their 'hearts' blood' for the people, for the cause. It is a tale of heroism, suffering and sacrifice; a tale of secret love, silently enduring. A tale and a dream that may one day come true.

This tale is about a little girl who sees that she is the odd one out in a family of beautiful people, people of heroic stature who can achieve marvellous things. She is of little consequence, an idle day-dreamer. Her one gift is love. She can love them with all her heart and help them to achieve their goals. This is her secret, her life's task: the sacrifice that is no sacrifice, having as she sees it nothing better to do. And her reward will be their love and gratitude, and basking in their reflected glory. Her happiness will be in making others happy, which as she has often been told is the true happiness. But the tale is never told, the secret remains undiscovered. She holds on to it, can't let it go because she doesn't know what else to do. And the dream dies unrealized. It is that sort of dream.)

Part I

'And the abyss?
It's right where you are —
A step down the stair'

Theodore Roethke

i

Underneath the fabric of my childhood and youth, like a dark and tortuous river, ran a deep channel, steeply carving a way through the rock-hard earth and the ocean bed. It was bottomless I knew. It contained unnameable dread; it contained despair, and death, or at least the opposite of life.

I say I knew, but in fact I didn't, or perhaps I was too afraid to admit that I knew. I knew about the awful dread that has no name, no shape, no face, no reason. It haunted me at night when I couldn't sleep. It was always there in the dark just out of sight. I didn't know what despair was. In fact what I felt was more a kind of resignation. As children do I accepted the way things were as the way they were meant to be.

It had all happened already. I had almost died, I should have died. It would have been easier all round if I had. I would not have known anything about it. But by some fluke, some mischance I had not. And so all that was left was the time in between, waiting until death caught up with me and fulfilled its purpose. But this time I would feel the pain and know the anguish.

I can't say how I knew that death would be so terrible. I knew that I had nearly died when I was a baby, and that I had been saved by my mother's devotion. In analysis I have re-experienced the pain and the loneliness. I suppose I thought all death would be like that.

If you had talked to me then I would not have told you any of this. I had not articulated it to myself, and in any case it concerned two taboo subjects: fear and death. I would expect to be scolded for having such morbid thoughts. Fear was not just cowardly, it was not even allowed to exist. So whenever I was afraid, and that was often, I kept it to myself

5

and stayed very still, hoping it would go away, or at least remain undetected. This produced a kind of paralysis that gave the appearance of sang-froid, and acquired for me a reputation for bravery among my friends that was quite unjustified.

I was nine years old when fear first came to stay. On that particular day my brother and I had gone to the cinema with my aunt, a rare treat, to see one of the first all-talking, all-singing, all-dancing films. First came the newsreel: pictures of the funeral of Sir Oliver Lodge, a well-known Spiritualist, followed by a seance to get in touch with him beyond the grave as he had promised they would be able to do. In a bare room on a circle of wooden chairs his sad-faced family – widow and children – and in the centre the medium, in a trance, head thrown back, eyes closed. The naked electric light bulb above her head began to swing violently back and forth, almost hitting her. She opened her mouth and a man's voice issued, harsh and gravelly. I don't remember what was said, only the deep incongruous sound. I was terrified. My aunt reassured me, bought me an ice-cream and held my hand until the pleasures of the film drove the fear from my mind. But that night when I went to bed I began to shake and couldn't stop, not knowing why until Mother, back from her meeting, asked my brother if anything had upset me during the day. He mentioned the seance and it all came flooding back. I was afraid that ghosts and spirits would come back from the dead to haunt me. Mother dismissed that briskly as a lot of nonsense: there are no ghosts. And anyway, she said on a more reassuring note, if her mother, who had died when I was five, were to come back it wouldn't be frightening because she was a nice woman. But comfort was only temporary.

From that day on I lived in constant fear. It was winter and began to get dark around four in the afternoon. Wherever I was, usually in school, I would begin to feel uneasy. A weight of dread would settle on my shoulders, and looking up to the high windows of the classroom I would see the light dimming as twilight approached and be consumed by fear. I would run all the way home, arriving breathless, rushing into warmth, light and safety. 'Who's chasing you?' Mother would ask, laughing at me.

At first I tried to talk to her about it, but her initial sympathy soon turned to impatience. She had told me there was nothing to be afraid of; it seemed wilful of me to continue. I must not allow myself to be afraid. She believed in the power of mind over matter. She was not afraid of anything. 'Life is an adventure, a challenge.' Its difficulties were there to be overcome, a task she performed with energy and gusto. I thought she was the bravest person I knew.

I remember feeling very alone. I would never again be able to say to anyone, I'm frightened. They would only tell me not to be. I could tell myself that. The battle against fear was mine; I would have to fight it alone. It was shameful to be afraid. Gradually the worst of the fear receded. For the rest I perfected a pretence. If I was afraid only I knew. That was the best I could manage.

Death was different, not so easily dismissed. Even Mother couldn't deny death, though I think she'd have liked to. But I knew children who had died, of diphtheria mostly, the prevalent disease of that time. They lived in our street. I had played with them.

When I was seven I had scarlet fever and nearly died a second time.

The Isolation Hospital was typical of its kind: huge and bare and depressingly ugly: long high wards, iron bedsteads, cold polished floors. The children with headlice had their heads shaved. I escaped that indignity. We found a dubious comfort in our view of the diphtheria block, separated from us by a high wire-mesh fence. They were going to die, we were not – or so we thought. We used to shout this at them when we were out for a walk until nurse made us stop; I don't think they heard us. Breakfast was always eggs, hard-boiled and usually cold, with thick slabs of white bread we called doorsteps. I hated both for a long time.

Mother would have nursed me at home, but my father worked at the docks and couldn't go to work while there was a danger of his carrying the infection; so I had to be removed. Just for a couple of weeks, Mother said. Three months later, feeling abandoned and miserable I was still in hospital. The nurses said I was too ill to go home. Mother said, soon. I didn't understand what was going on. One day I would be up, helping with the distribution of meals, play-ing, going for walks in the grounds. The next, in what seemed an arbitrary manner, I was back in bed, ill again they said. I learned later that each time a child was admitted I caught their germs.

At Christmastime a tall fir tree stood in the centre of the ward. Presents arrived daily and were stacked around it. We made paper chains and the nurses festooned the walls with them. All the girls coveted the fairy doll on the top of the tree: blonde, blue-eyed, beautiful. On Christmas day I was up, fully dressed, excited. The hospital governors came and the presents were distributed. My mother was chairman of the governors, but she was not there. I suppose she was cooking Christmas dinner for the rest of the family. As Mother's representative I stood politely by, awaiting my turn to be given a present from the tree. Around me children jumped up and down and shouted with excitement. After what seemed an interminable time but probably wasn't, the tree was bare, the ground littered with paper, the noise somewhat subdued and I still stood rooted to the ground, stiff with inarticulate misery. The fairy doll had gone, to a little girl who had just come in and was very ill. 'How sad,' they said, 'to have to come into hospital on Christmas day.' Finally one of the governors noticed me. 'What have you got?' he asked kindly, 'Haven't you got a present?' I shook my head. They searched among the debris and found a toy violin with a broken bow and handed it to me. They knew I wouldn't mind. I had plenty of toys. I said thank you.

I don't remember any more until the next day. I was in bed again. Mother and Matron were sitting beside me. Mother had given me a doll, a replacement for my favourite rag doll that a wicked nurse had sent to the incinerator. It lay untouched on my bed. I was not interested. Something very strange was happening. Mother was crying. I had never seen her cry. I felt I should comfort her, reach out my hand, tell her I liked the doll, tell her not to cry, as she would tell me. But I couldn't be bothered, couldn't make the effort. Everything seemed very far away and I couldn't hear what they were saying.

Next thing I remember I was in the isolation ward, where we went to be disinfected before going home, and very excited. My ears were still leaking wax, and the nurse said I had no hope of going home until they stopped. 'I am, I am,' I cried desperately.

This time my faith in Mother was justified, and I was soon being propelled in a push-chair past a phalanx of disapproving nurses out into the free fresh air and home, defying the express edicts of the hospital doctors. Mother said I would have died if she had left me there any longer. Our family doctor told her I would not have been able to withstand indefinitely the constantly renewed infection. For the second time I owed my life to Mother.

Thinking about it later I decided that it must have been on Boxing Day when Mother made up her mind to take me home. That would be when I nearly died. That was why she was crying. That explained how I felt too and why everything seemed so far away. That must be how it felt to die. I was glad of course that she had saved me, but that was the first time I thought seriously about death. It would have been quite easy and painless if I had died then. I had not been frightened because I didn't know I was dying. When many years later I gave this view of things, which I had seen no reason to alter, for the first time to another person, Dr Penny my analyst, she looked rather sceptical. She didn't think I had been dying then, and if I was dying of anything it was most likely to be of frustrated rage, and that was why I couldn't talk to my mother or comfort her. She also thought I must have had a strong constitution. That was probably what saved my life as much as anything. Mother the life-saver debunked! It was almost sacrilegious. I expected at least a shaft of lightning to strike her down.

My thoughts about this did not seem to me either morbid or strange. I thought I was being sensible. I suppose I was trying to come to terms with my fears and with the reality of death. But I never talked to anyone about it. It would have been better if I had died when I was a baby. But as I hadn't, and hadn't again a second time, that was that; I had to get on with it and make the best of it. In a photograph taken that summer I am standing on the steps leading down to the garden, smiling a tense, tight-lipped smile. That is partly because I was trying not to open my mouth and show my teeth which someone had said were too big. I used to smile a lot. I think my parents saw the smile but not the effort it cost. My brother stands next to me on one leg scowling into the sun. He rarely smiled, especially in photographs.

Sometimes it hardly seemed worthwhile: a lot to get through and the abyss waiting. It was like walking a tightrope across Niagara Falls knowing what one false step will do.

*

It wasn't always like that. I can remember a time when I fitted snugly into the world. I was very small and looked after by my very large parents, who kept me safe.

Before I was old enough to attend school we used to go to Canvey Island for our summer holidays. Where we stayed there weren't any proper roads. Only grassy fields, the cliffs

10

and the sea always a long way out. I remember walking towards it across the mud flats holding my father's hand and sitting on his shoulders as he strode into it unafraid. Up the lane there was a big Alsatian dog. It used to bark every time I went by and rush towards me. It was on a long chain so there was no danger. But I was always afraid it would get loose. One year the bungalow, which had been recommended by someone from my father's work, wasn't very clean and I got bitten by bed bugs all over and we had to go home. We didn't go there again. One year it rained a lot. There was mud everywhere. Mother and I went down to inspect the new bungalow and make sure it was clean. We walked back across the fields to the station. Thunderclouds were gathering in the sky ahead and being twisted into sinister shapes by a fierce wind. I was frightened and couldn't stop crying. Mother made me turn and walk backwards so that I could look at the sun setting in a still clear blue sky behind us. Each time I turned to the front I started to cry again. I don't think I would have remembered that had it not entered the annals of family history as a funny story. How easy it was to bamboozle me. And how clever of Mother to stop me crying.

My grandmother came to visit us. It was so muddy that my father had to carry her from the car to our bungalow. She didn't have any wellington boots. She was rather large and he was rather small; they looked very funny. I learned a poem:

> John had a great big mackintosh coat on,
> John had a great big mackintosh hat.
> John had great big wellington boots on,
> And that, said John, is that.

I remember a man with a concertina and a tiny monkey with mournful eyes perched on his shoulder rattling a tin cup. And I remember the smell of the sea and the mud and the satisfying feel of it.

Mother and I, twin souls. Somehow I knew without ever putting it into words, even in my thoughts, how fragile she was under her tough, undaunted exterior. She must not be wounded, she must not be disbelieved or even doubted. I once dared to call her silly. She was so upset I never did it again. It was a paradox. This mother whose strength I relied on to keep me safe, whose wrath I feared, and whom I obeyed instantly, was the same mother whose frailties I had to care for and protect. I always wanted to please her, win her approval and her love. But I also knew how easily hurt she was; when someone was unkind to her I saw her turn pale and felt the pain she was never able to express.

One incident sums it all up.

I was five. It was New Year. I know Christmas was not long past because my presents were still downstairs where I could see and delight in them every moment. Soon they would be banished to the bedroom and the realm of ordinary toys. But for now they were still in the corner of the kitchen (unfortunately as it turned out): the new cot and the most beautiful china doll. The best thing about the new doll was her accessibility. She was smarter and more beautiful than my other dolls, but she was not so big nor so awfully expensive as my very best doll who only came out on Sundays. (She came from Paris, brought by an aunt.) I would be able to play with this one. She was called Sylvia.

Mother's brother, my Uncle Frank, his wife and small daughter Julie were staying with us while they waited for a boat that would take them to Australia. They were emigrating because Uncle Frank could not find work here. Grandpa had had to sell his farm during the war because his sons were in the army and he had no one to help him; Frank hadn't worked since. They were going to seek their fortune. An older brother and sister were out there already. I liked Uncle Frank; he played games with us and let me sit on his knee. Mother said he was her favourite brother.

Everyone was cheerful, but I knew that underneath they were all sad, especially my mother. On the day they were leaving the sadness in the house was palpable, like a weight in the air that made everyone move around quietly and talk in hushed tones. Their luggage was in the hall; they sat with their coats and hats on waiting for the taxicab. Even Julie was miserable; she who was usually far too boisterous and bossy for my liking, even if she was a year older than me. She stayed close to her mother and held on to her coat as if she was afraid of being left behind. The waiting was intolerable and interminable. We couldn't even go outside to play.

Suddenly Mother said, 'Why don't you give Julie one of your dolls to take on her journey?'

Polite protests from Uncle Frank and Aunty Trudy over-ridden by Mother. 'She has a lot of dolls – too many,' and to me, 'You won't mind, will you?'

I considered. I loved all my dolls dearly, but although I didn't like her much I did feel sorry for Julie. I knew they were very poor, and she didn't seem to have any toys at all. Australia was a long way away; not very nice to have no one to cuddle in bed all that time on a big boat.

'No, I don't mind, but which one?' I was pondering.

'Oh you can't give her one of your old dolls, they're too worn and dirty.'

They weren't.

'Give her your new doll.'

I was stunned. A profound sense of shock, plus well-drilled politeness, kept me silent: a silence which was taken for acquiescence.

Everyone suddenly cheered up. Julie's eyes shone as she hugged her new acquisition tightly. All the grown-ups were smiling, and tongues that had fallen silent loosened and became suddenly voluble. In the hubbub my silence was unnoticed.

'What shall I call her?' asked Julie. 'I know, I'll call her after you, then I'll always remember you.'

'What a nice idea,' said my treacherous mother.

She has a name, I wanted to shout, she's called Sylvia; but I didn't, I said nothing. My dislike of Julie intensified. I hated her.

Mother was smiling at me. I knew she was pleased with me. Inside my head an outraged voice was saying loud and clear, 'I'm only five.' But what can you do when you see how happy you've made everyone, and you know how easily that happiness can be destroyed?

We lived in a council house at the top end of the road, a position that indicated our standing relative to the other people in the road. It was never openly stated but I knew. We were different and we were superior. We had to be. It would have been unbearable just to be different. My father was discharged from the army at the end of the First World War with a wife and one child – my brother – no money and nowhere to live. At first they lived with my grandparents, but that didn't work. The family (i.e. Greatgrandmother) didn't approve of Mother's feminist ideas. So as soon as they began building them, my father applied for a council house.

I was born there and we lived there until I was twelve. I hated it though I didn't realise that I did until we had moved. But everywhere I went I picked out houses that I wanted to live in when I grew up. They were always what I called proper houses: double-fronted and standing in their own grounds. My fantasies stopped short of the really grand estate – not that I wouldn't have liked to live on one – but I couldn't imagine where I would get the money to pay the servants. Also as a good socialist I would have had to turn it over to the state. My parents would have been shocked to know what a little snob I was. It nearly broke my mother's heart when she heard herself described as 'that middle-class woman', and my father was always oblivious to his surroundings as long as he had a comfortable chair to sit in and his meals ready on the table when he came home from work.

Our superiority was not obvious. Our differences were. My father was one of the lucky ones who had a steady job and the prospect of a pension. Half the street had husbands who were in and out of work through no fault of their own, and when they were unemployed only the prospect of ten shillings a week to keep a whole family.

Mr Tomson next door was an engine driver, when in work, with five children, one of them a son who was a mongol, as they were called then. Nothing could be done for him, but he was much loved. 'A child of God.' Some holy-roller relatives used to take him to church for healing prayers. And he would delight us all by mounting a wooden box and re-enacting the sermon with flailing arms and uncanny accuracy considering he used no words, only a passionate crescendo of cries and sounds.

I took him for walks. I've no idea why, since he was bigger than me. He would infuriate and embarrass me by sitting down in the middle of the road and refusing to move however much I tugged and pleaded. The traffic had to go round us. He once got me into terrible trouble. In response to his pestering I let him hold one of my best dolls. He cradled it tenderly and crooned to it, then suddenly tiring of it threw it down on to the pavement where it shattered, being made of china. I was very upset, my dolls were like people to me. I hit him and he ran howling to his mother. I was in deep disgrace with my mother. I should have known better than to let him hold it. And what was I doing with that doll out in the street in the first place? But Mrs Tomson was on my side. (She usually was.)

I think that must have been the starting point of my career as a remedial teacher. He died of pneumonia when he was fourteen. Everyone said it was a blessing.

Mother used to give Mrs Tomson the dripping from our

weekend joint and sweets for the children. She was too proud to take anything more. I remember it particularly as I was very fond of dripping myself; it was a real sacrifice. And I was forbidden to accept any food when I was in their house playing with my friend Jean, their daughter. That wasn't difficult as it was only ever thick chunks of bread and strong cups of tea. I didn't like either.

I learned about disadvantage early and at first hand. When Mother stood for the council almost every house in the road bloomed with red and yellow cards bearing her name. One of the few exceptions was the house of the people opposite who spoke to no one and were rumoured to vote Conservative. I don't even remember what they looked like. There was a high privet hedge around their front garden and outside in the road was the only car in the neighbourhood. One of the dares in our evening games was to knock on their front door and run away.

My school friends had carpets, antimacassars and a lot of knick-knacks. We had dark linoleum, one carpet in the sitting room, no ornaments – they make work – and what my friends called rude pictures: reproductions of Greek and Roman statuary and a sepia tint of September Morn: a nude woman bathing in a lake modestly covering most of the rude bits. Their clothes followed the fashion; mine were serviceable, and for best, dresses made by Aunt Maria (who had been trained by a court dressmaker) and unlike anyone else's. They were lovely dresses but I hated wearing them. I wanted to look like everyone else.

Our superiority, in my eyes that is, came from knowing that our way of life was superior. Mother and Father didn't waste money on inessentials: we had a healthy but frugal diet – never more than half an apple each – we went camping at weekends and had a summer holiday – only camping which was cheap – but most of my friends couldn't afford even that; we read books, and my brother and I were expected to win scholarships for further education. The boys next door won scholarships to the grammar school too but couldn't afford to stay on past fifteen. By the time I got to the sixth form none of my friends were still at school. There were only six of us altogether. We were girls of course; education was meant for boys.

Most importantly we were out to change the world for the better. My vision of how the future should be was derived from the ideas of William Morris, as recounted to me by Mother: everyone singing and dancing and making beautiful things in eternal green fields.

The knowledge of being superior didn't make me happy. It was something to live by and aspire to, but I didn't want to be different, I didn't like the jeering of boys at the way we looked with our shorts and rucksacks going to camp. Only the boy scouts wore shorts then. And I didn't like having to stand up for my principles. But I felt a traitor when I didn't. As Mother used to say, 'Dare to be a Daniel.' Although she had rejected her parents' God her conversation was still larded with biblical wisdom.

That was another thing. I was the only girl in my class who hadn't been christened.

'You've got to believe in God. You'll go to hell if you don't.'

'No I won't. There isn't a God. You can't prove there is.'

'Who made the world then? My mum says I shouldn't play with you if you don't believe in God.'

'Well if there is a God who made him then?' End of argument.

Friends' mothers were very shocked if they discovered that I didn't say my prayers. One of them refused to let her daughter come camping with us because we didn't go to church on Sunday. I was very proud of my parents, but I didn't know anyone else who had parents who stood on the corner of the High Street making speeches and getting heckled and entering into arguments with complete strangers.

Mother was a natural leader. The women in the street brought their troubles to her and their minor illnesses. TCP for sore throats and bicarbonate for indigestion, various herbal remedies for skin complaints and bowels. No one went to the doctor then unless they were seriously ill, and sometimes not even then.

I loved camping and I loved the marches to Hyde Park and the May Day festivities, singing pacifist and socialist songs and shouting slogans: 'No more war. Scholarships not battleships. Butter not bombs. Chamberlain must go (accompanied by a rude gesture). I was filled with fervour and good intentions. But my schoolfriends were mostly good working-class Tories. When we had a mock parliament in school and I was the Labour candidate I had one supporter. I couldn't be like them, my friends. But how I wished I could. I knew they were wrong but it was lonely being the only one in the right. And I was a coward.

iii

When I was six my parents joined the Woodcraft Folk, an organization for young people – and others of any age; whole families may join, as we did. It is affiliated to the Cooperative movement, and was begun in the 1920s by Leslie Paul, with the idea of introducing working-class children to a more natural and healthy way of life. In those days working-class children in the city had hardly seen a tree or a cow – milk came in bottles. It also aimed to impart socialist principles, although it wasn't affiliated to any political party. Every weekend in the summer we went camping, and in the winter what was then called 'hiking'. At camp we lived as simply and as close to nature as possible: sleeping in small tents, cooking over open fires. In the evening we gathered round a huge campfire and sang songs, danced, play-acted and told stories. We learned handicrafts, we made our own costumes. Many of our activities are now part of the school curriculum.

But then it was a new and alternative way of life, previously the prerogative of the wealthy and the leisured.

We were taught a respect for the earth and all its creatures, including man, a philosophy akin to that of the North American Indians: a kinship with all living things. The earth gave us its bounty, and its beauty; for our part we were to make use of it, to care for it and help in its renewal. We were concerned about ecology long before anyone had even heard of it. Farmers liked us because we didn't damage their crops or tease their animals; we left the fields as we found them: all litter was collected and burnt, every divot of turf carefully replaced. I led two lives: one as a schoolgirl taught to cover my legs, to dress modestly, to sit with my knees closed and my hands in my lap, to walk not run, to behave decorously and work hard; the other, which came to feel like my real life, every weekend and for longer periods in the summer, dressed any-old-how, most often in shorts or swimsuit, with delirious freedom to run and play and shout and sing and work – and in the open air work often felt like play – and do not only the boring things that girls were supposed to do but the same as the boys. For that was another great boon: there were boys to work with, play with, fight with, fall in love with, and all on an equal basis. It was a world apart; our separation from the everyday emphasised by an initiation ceremony in which we chose a new name from nature, from folklore or myth. At Woodcraft camps and meetings we were known only by our chosen name. The air resounded with 'Panther and Tiger, Willow and Marigold, Redflower and Otter, Owasa and Swift Canoe, Onaway and Calumet'.

At camp my parents too were different. It was liberating for them, momentarily away from work and responsibility, more relaxed than I ever saw them at home. Which seems odd when I think about it. They had thirty or forty of other people's children to look after. But as a child myself I didn't see that as a responsibility.

Mother became the first 'Headman'; Father learned to

cook. Dad could indulge the romantic, adventurous, creative side of himself that was atrophied in a boring office job. We acted in plays that he wrote, we danced to tunes from his penny whistle. For Mother the greatest thing was rest, to let others take the strain, do the work while she relaxed, share some of the burden that she always felt so heavy on her shoulders. She usually began the weekend looking exhausted, having packed and organized everything, and gradually revived.

Much of my sense of freedom derived from the distance I was able to put between myself and Mother. With my peers I was just one of the crowd, doing my best to belong, joining in, especially with anything forbidden: scrumping for apples, midnight feasts, moonlight walks discovering the strange esoteric world of the night, and later other pleasures; taking advantage of opportunities that never arose at home.

But with my father the opposite was true. At home I saw little of him. When he wasn't at work he was out at meetings, and when he was at home he was not to be disturbed. It was Mother who took care of us. Father provided the bread and the roof, and, as he said, an occasional kindly pat on the head. So I saw more of him at camp, and in some ways he was more accessible; I got to know a different side of him. I adored him and thought him the most handsome man in the world, but I was only one of thirty or more children he was in charge of. I got no favours, nor expected any, and I never had him to myself.

My Woodcraft experience made a 'groupie' of me. I feel at home in a group, and expect, as others do not, that the group will look after me. I was for a long time the youngest member of our Woodcraft group, and all the older boys and girls took care of me, played with me, and made a great fuss of me. All our activities playful or serious took place in groups, and all our decisions were group decisions.

The blessings for me were manifold. There I was truly another person. The experience of being in the heart of a natural world: the beauty of it that awed me, the sense of its mystery that excited me, the physical freedom and the activity that fulfilled and healthily tired my body. There was a sense of camaraderie, of common purpose that came from living with a group of like-minded though very different and individual people. The Woodcraft Folk attracted the idiosyncratic, the eccentric, the misfit.

The war cut me off from it. But its impact on me has been lifelong and of vital importance to my survival and my sanity. The Woodcraft Folk was my 'Jesuit'; it provided me with a religious experience − though it was never called that, and such an idea would have horrified my rational humanist parents − that became and has remained a fundamental part of me.

I was a nervous child, but much less so at camp. At home in a safely locked house the dark was full of menace. Lying close to the earth in an open field it was never completely dark; I could see the sky and the stars, feel the wind on my cheek, and I was rarely afraid. Many years later at a time of great personal stress I lived opposite a stretch of common land, a part of London's green belt. Whenever I was troubled I walked out across the grass, preferably at night when no one was around. Standing under the trees my troubles drained away, and a feeling of rightness and of belonging spread through me. The earth itself renewed me: its timelessness, its impersonality, its lack of judgement, its lack of caring even. There it was and ever had been, and there for a while was I, lost but finding in its heart a safe haven.

*

I was still seven, very nearly eight, in the days when a year was a long time, alone with my father − Mother presumably out at a meeting − climbing on to his knee, to lean against his broad chest, take his watch out of his waistcoat pocket and listen to it tick and cajole him into telling me a story before I went to bed. He told lovely stories, funny exciting stories that he made up. But he was always reluctant and had to be persuaded quite hard to tell them as often as I wanted to hear them.

But this evening, to my shocked surprise, he pushed me abruptly from his knee and stood up, saying quite impatiently, in contrast to his usual good temper, 'You're getting too old for that.'

'But why?'

'You're a big girl now, and big girls don't sit on their daddy's knee.' He went on, 'And big girls don't get told stories.'

I must have looked upset – I don't remember that I said anything – for he seemed to feel that I needed an explanation. 'Real life isn't about fairy stories. Real life is hard. It's about working hard and having to fight for justice and fair play. Like your mother and I do. "Life is real! Life is earnest!" ' That was the first, but not the last time that I heard that quotation, as well as the other one that I came to dislike equally, about putting away 'childish things'.

I must have continued to look upset because he relented a little. 'I will tell you one last story. But it is a real story about a real boy who spent his life working hard to help other people.' And he told me the story of Keir Hardie, the miner's son who became the first working-class MP. I sat on the floor and listened very solemnly and with dignity. I felt privileged; my father was treating me like a grown-up.

He kept to his word. He never told me another story, and I never again attempted to sit on his knee.

That was the end of my childhood.

iv

Adolescence was a time of opening out, a time of hope. It was about boys and falling in love, which I did all the time. The path ahead was clear: school and a career, love and marriage. Those two aims were difficult to reconcile in an era when marriage automatically ended most women's careers. But it was a new age, everything was possible; maybe I would have both. I was busy living I thought, but perhaps only being carried along by the stream of events and a large element of wishful thinking. It was an exciting and inspiring time. There was an upsurge of political idealism as the world prepared for its battle between good and evil. Amid the burgeoning of fascism we clung to our belief in Utopia. The issues were clear: fascist oppression must be ended; everyone must have an adequate standard of living. I had not yet learned enough of the intransigence of human nature to make me doubt the likelihood of achieving these to me simple goals. I believed in progress and in the perfectibility of man. Like plants given the right environment people would bloom and grow in understanding and health. Education was the key.

But as the psychiatrist said to the light bulb, you have to want to change. There was no doubt about the existence of evil oppression. But although difficult to find now, there were plenty who admired Nazi efficiency and ignored the rest or thought it exaggerated. We knew: at international youth camps we met refugees and heard their stories. There was a vivid reminder of what they had left behind at the Woodcraft international camp on the South Downs in 1937 when an ordinary little plane flew over, and the Spanish children, all refugees, flattened themselves on the ground. Austrian and German Jews and socialists were found places to live in sympathetic homes, such as ours, becoming part of the family until the war made them aliens and they vanished into detention camps.

I believed the suffering of the refugees, but still expected that Fascism would be defeated, and Utopia miraculously would follow. When that time came I too would be transformed. Like all the unhappy girls in fairy stories, Cinderella would have her prince and her happy ending. Magically all would be well – even in a world preparing for war!

How unrealistic it all seems now. Privately other lessons were being learned. But they were painful and I tried to banish them from my memory – and almost succeeded. It is hard to live without hope.

Memories surface with difficulty. I'm reluctant to recall them. Naked emotions of the kind that assailed me in my teens were distasteful, embarrassing other people, making them uncomfortable; deservedly ridiculed. I learned to be the first to laugh, to laugh at myself before they did. 'Laugh and the world laughs with you' – a platitude but true. I didn't want to 'weep alone'.

It was a joke when I wept at being parted from my true love. He was twelve and so was I: a choirboy with a beautiful face and a beautiful voice. It was a joke whenever I showed my feelings. By the time I was eighteen I had learned to hide them. It took longer to lose them altogether.

It made no difference what the emotion was; it was the extreme nature of it and its expression. Whether I was starry-eyed and speechless over one of my many idols, who might be Gary Cooper or Paul Robeson, Krishna Menon or our local MP, or devastated by a sad story, a poem or a song, such feelings were taboo, foolish and unnecessary; better hidden. 'You're too sensitive, too thin-skinned. You take things too seriously.' The leitmotif for most of my life.

'If it makes you cry don't read it': Mother at my reaction to the death of Little Nell.

My father, on the occasion of a public speech by our MP

at the town-hall, when I sat on the platform with my parents: 'If you could have seen your face! Your mouth open – or if it wasn't it might as well have been. You couldn't take your eyes off him – mooning over him like a love-sick maiden – everyone could see.' He laughed. I was mortified. How could I be so naïve?

Mother smiled, 'You don't want everyone to see do you?'

My brother, as usual on these occasions, said nothing. Probably glad that I was under discussion and not he. He was sometimes over emotional, but he was artistic so allowances could be made.

I was never any good at domestic science, hated it; disliked and despised the domestic-science teacher Miss Townsend, and she in turn disliked and whenever possible ignored me. If praise was due it went to my partner; the blame was mine. I avoided her lessons whenever I could. We were divided into two groups and alternated: art one week, domestic science the next. Except when the art teacher got suspicious and sent me back to the kitchen, I stayed in her more kindly orbit. I wasn't any good at art either but she never criticised; commenting only that I worked harder with my tongue than my pencil. If Miss T noticed my absence she never queried it.

At primary school I had excelled at sewing and knitting and embroidery. At home my fairy cakes were said to be delicious. Mother was chairman of the governing body of my grammar school; that brought me not one advantage that I could see. A tendency on the part of some teachers to regard me benignly whatever I did, was counterbalanced by others who were always sure that I was about to take advantage of my privileged position. It was difficult for me to believe in the disinterest of my teachers' judgements. Likewise it was hard for the other girls not to regard me as unfairly privileged. But one thing was sure. Mother knew the school rules. No one could take advantage of us; in contrast to most of my friends, whose parents usually rushed to comply with the teachers' demands. Even the most-feared headmistress was routed by Mother and me.

A first-former, quaking in my shoes, I was called out from the anonymity of my class as we stood in disciplined lines in the cold playground.

'Why are you not wearing stockings? Young ladies' legs should always be covered. You don't want people to see your knees, do you?'

'Please Miss Edwards, my mother says we don't have to wear stockings until we're twelve.'

'And you are?'

'Eleven and nine months.'

'And your mother is?'

'Mrs Hargreaves, Miss Edwards,' head modestly bowed.

A highly charged silence. Then graciously, 'Of course, your mother is quite right. You are a big girl for your age. I shall be looking out for you on your birthday.' And she was.

Miss Edwards knew when to admit defeat. Others did not, Miss T among them, or at least not so gracefully.

'You will bring a fillet of fish to your next lesson and I will show you how to bake it.' Miss T to the class.

'You will do no such thing,' said my mother. 'The school is supposed to supply all the ingredients you need. Whatever the other girls do, to send you along with a piece of fish is to encourage Miss Townsend's laziness, and would be breaking the rules. Not every mother can afford to buy fish for cookery lessons, or whatever else Miss T demands.'

So the following day, the only fishless girl, I stood my ground and repeated once more: 'My mother says . . .'

Oh stupid Miss T, oh unkind Miss T who, humiliated and outfaced, could not see that I was only the messenger, assumed my complicity and triumph, and set me, being without fish, to do all the washing up and wiping down, and never willingly addressed another word to me in the next four years.

A more public humiliation concerned Greek tunics. In the first year we did gymnastics and games in our jumpers and navy blue knickers. But after that a garment which more decently covered us was considered desirable. This, a copy of a Greek tunic, black and shapeless, was flattering to no one and not part of the official uniform. So parents were asked to provide them, which most of them grumblingly did. Except of course my mother who objected on behalf of all those, including herself, who couldn't afford this unnecessary extra.

This time Mother met her match – I expect prudery won the day – and she was outvoted. For a term I was a source of irritation to the gym teacher, old Stumps, until Mother gave in and harmony was restored. Old Stumps never blamed me for Mother's shortcomings. Not even when worse transpired. I lost my tunic. I left it in the cloakroom and it disappeared. Mother believed me. Stumps said it must be replaced. Mother refused; it had been lost on school property, the school was responsible, the school should replace it. Stalemate.

Older by three years and by now used to this and more thick-skinned I did gym in my knickers while all around had their bottoms decently covered. To her eternal credit, and tempted though I'm sure she was, old Stumps did not take it out on me. But that I was an abomination in her sight is without doubt. She tolerated, no, put up with the situation for a term and then brought the whole school to a standstill. If my tunic had been lost in school then it must still be there. The school must be searched and each tunic accounted for. This was easier than it sounds as all our belongings had to be marked with our names. The cloakrooms were cleared and all our things taken to our classrooms, piled high on our desks. I was not very happy, but while my friends sympathised with my predicament, even my enemies welcomed the break from lessons, and I sensed a kind of awe in the sideways glances at the cause of such total upheaval. The prefects searched the cloakrooms and all the communal parts of the school. Finally my tunic, dusty and very crumpled, was discovered stuffed down behind one of the radiators. I was vindicated. Mother was vindicated. And old Stumps, outwardly a fierce, short-tempered dragon of whom we were all terrified, proved her innate kindliness by never holding it against either me or my mother. I think she enjoyed a good scrap even when she lost.

*

When I look back across the years, a picture emerges not of one person but two: one public, one private; one acceptable, one not. One was attractive, clever and quite popular. The other, the private one was fat and ugly, ignorant and stupid, lazy and deceitful, a cringing sycophant, a hypocrite, jealous, envious, easily hurt, very sad, very lonely.

The unacceptable one was packed in a trunk labelled 'Not wanted on voyage' and banished to the cellar. Not quite forgotten; I was always uneasily aware that there was a not-so-nice me that no one knew. She emerged occasionally in isolated, apparently motiveless episodes. With a friend from an impeccable middle-class family one summer evening idly wandering, deciding to explore a large, unoccupied mansion; at the rear a lofty glass conservatory housing a tall vine. A casual stone, a satisfying crack and a cascade of falling glass escalated to an orgy of smashing, wilfully, gleefully, and eventually disturbing the neighbours who sent for the police. We escaped just in time to meet them in the street and pass them by demurely, two sixteen-year-old girls walking sedately along in school uniform – quite above suspicion.

The dichotomy that helped me to avoid public humiliation when my boyfriend danced with another girl, also stopped me finding out that the girl was his sister. I was too busy dancing with someone else, showing him I didn't care.

At college I acquired a reputation as a 'social butterfly',

hard and uncaring. (Shades of my mother always shrugging off my father's affectionate arm: 'Oh, go on with you.') Head high, chin up, nose in the air, who cares? But I did. The formula worked up to a point – but left everything that mattered unresolved.

A silly song – 'Green leaves are green, green leaves are green, green leaves are gre-een, green leaves are green. Chorus: *Bluebells are blue, bluebells are blue, bluebells are blu-ue, bluebells are blue.* Chorus: Green leaves are green . . . , etc.' – to be repeated *ad infinitum. Ad nauseam* to our unwilling audience.

We sang it at every opportunity, mostly at camp, and on any or no pretext at all. It brings back being sixteen with a pungent sharpness. When I hear it I can smell the damp grass, hear the snapping of wintery twigs as we forced our way into the forest and see the deep blue of the bluebells that covered the open ground and spread under the trees in a blazing carpet. The raindrops on the bushes that we disturbed in passing soaked through our thick jumpers and our woollen socks.

But in a strange way it was not a silly song at all. Its nursery-like repetition expressed our adolescent feelings perfectly. What more could we say? Spring returns again and the grass is green, the bluebells are blue. We sang the joy of being young and alive as we roamed the woods and the fields; we sang our hearts out.

But it also brings back with an undertow of sadness the embarrassment and awkwardness of being sixteen. My body which suddenly looked grown-up and attracted men who thought I was older. Spud – everyone called him that, I've no idea why, but it's the only name I remember – was nineteen, working class, seriously interested in politics and in me, and attractive in a physically immediate way that was quite different from the gangling uncertain boys I was used to. He fascinated and terrified me. He invited me to spend a day in the forest with him. My mind boggled at what that might mean, and terror won out. Imagining I was playing it sophisticated, I said, 'My mother said I never should play with the gypsies in the wood.' It didn't sound as funny as I meant it to. He saw only snobbish rejection and was very hurt and angry. He never spoke to me again. I wish I would have explained but I didn't know how. It was impossible to tell him how frightened I was.

The year I was sixteen was the year of the Spanish Civil War and our first aquaintance with refugees and the horrors of war. It's not surprising that we resisted growing up, as some of our elders bitterly complained. We played childish games: 'Poor Jenny is a-weeping', and had what we called 'bundles', a kind of communal fight and free for all usually started by one boy jumping on another. The boys pelted the girls with clods of earth. The girls retaliated by letting the boys' tents down and removing the pegs.

We lived under the shadow of war which seemed increasingly unavoidable. The war from which some of the boys I played with did not return.

V

Marriage did end my career, if you can call two years of teaching a career. I had survived the war. But there had been no transformation.

For six years life had been on hold, all my energy focused on getting through, on getting by. Everything was explained and excused in one simple phrase, 'There's a war on.'

At first the war was experienced as a lack, a deprivation: of my brother who was abroad with the army medical corps and not seen for the whole six years; of food and clothing: ration books, queueing, make do and mend, getting used to dried eggs and weird kinds of meat – horse and whale – I preferred to do without; of men who suddenly disappeared from our classrooms at college leaving only a few graduates, among them my future husband Nick, and the physically unfit; a lack of heat and light and sleep: frozen feet and the blackout, nights in the cellar or the air-raid shelter. I was out of London a lot of the time at college so I missed the worst of the blitz, but I was regarded as a heroine for going back each holiday.

Then I began teaching: a haphazard introduction (with a nucleus of children who had stayed in London and those who had straggled back from evacuation), with little equipment and a lot of improvisation.

At lunch in a small café on my first day as a permanent class teacher (I had been a 'floater' till then) it occurred to me that this was going to be my life for the next possibly forty years: standing in front of a class every morning at nine a.m. Playtime was over. This was the reality. But this wasn't what I wanted to do with my life. What did I want? I didn't know. What else could I do? I supposed I would get used to it, I supposed I would get to like it as others seemed to. Why should I expect to be different from anyone else?

That was the first time, looking back, that I experienced real depression. Till then life had all been in the future. But I was young, I shook it off; anything might happen, and I was in love.

The last year of the war I spent evacuated with Jessica, my firstborn, in Berkshire, and had my first experience of being badly treated, of being disliked not for anything I had done but simply for being who I was: an evacuee from London – 'where things are not half so bad as they make out' – taking food out of the mouths of legitimate villagers. 'Why don't you go home?' No one spoke to me. Conversations stopped when I approached and resumed when I had passed just loud enough for me to hear what they thought of me. When I entered a shop goods disappeared under the counter and if produced were 'only for the regulars'. What do you expect? There's a war on.

With the end of the war and the returning soldiers came a tidal wave of passion for change, for a better life, for what we thought we had been fighting for, democracy and justice. We had won the war, we could win the peace.

I can remember no more solidly satisfying moment in my life than the night when the Labour Party for the first time in history swept to power with a large enough majority to make real change a possibility. Nick and I had turned our sitting room into a committee room. I organised canvassing rotas, leaflet folding and addressing and cups of tea for the footweary. It was a mild night. When the polls closed we sat on the iron staircase leading down to the back garden, laughing and cheering and annoying our Tory neighbours as we listened to the results on the radio – and getting intoxicated on tea and sandwiches.

But people were weary and tired of austerity, and couldn't sustain their vision of the promised land that didn't materialise immediately. Disillusion set in. It was then I lost my belief in ideal solutions. As I had suspected the Garden of Eden was a myth, and human beings remained fallible and imperfect, internally divided.

Harder to relinquish were my personal dreams.

The abyss was still there. Time was running out. I kept it at bay by filling every moment: with family, friends, good works, politics.

I lived in the future. One day, I consoled myself, everything will be all right: everything meaning society in general and my own life in particular. My children were the best reason and the best reward for being alive. Any leftover time, any unplanned-for space, empty nook or cranny I stuffed full of books, of which I read at least one a day and remembered nothing.

I confused life with activity, and mistook merit marks for meaning. If I worked hard enough and was good enough some big jailer-in-the-sky would let me off. That's a yawning pit. There aren't enough good deeds or kind thoughts to fill it. Survival seemed to be the point. But for what? I never stood still long enough to find out. Some undefined good time, some kind of fulfilment, a day when I could stop and not be frightened. I was on a treadmill going nowhere. Hope was fading and could no longer sustain me. I was bored, I was unhappy and increasingly frightened.

vi

And suddenly I was middle-aged. Resuming my 'career' had made no difference to my sense of failure. I had run out of excuses. Life was speeding past and something vital had eluded me. It was not what I had intended. Perhaps I hadn't tried hard enough. Nick had his own problems, he couldn't help me with mine.

A day came when the waters rose around me and fear engulfed me: fear of a crack in the pavement, of a puddle in the road; houses and buildings leaned towards me: portents, harbingers of disaster. Death waited outside in the street, tapped at the window, agitated the leaves on trees and bushes when the wind blew. At night I felt safe only when all my family were 'gathered in', curtains drawn and doors bolted. In the garden a cowled figure stood illumined by the moon-light. I couldn't see his face. He looked like a monk. He stood quite still. He frightened me. Even when I couldn't see him I knew he was there, waiting for me. (Years later I met him again at a workshop as one of the images in a visualizing exercise. He removed his cowl and I saw his head: a fleshless skull. He said his name was Death. He had been dead a long, long time.) My nightmares came true. The abyss opened at my feet and I fell, as I had always known someday

I would. I sank to the bottom of a seemingly bottomless pit . . . down and down, endlessly down.

At the bottom unexpectedly the strongest sensation was relief. I could fall no further. Effort was over. Striving was over. It was unnecessary. Down here there is nothing to strive for. Down here there is time, endless time and no time at all; no distractions, no friends; nobody wants to join you. You can sit here for ever, or at least until you want to move. To do something because you want to, not because you must, is a novel idea. At the bottom you are safe. If there's nothing to distract you − and that's hard to live with − you can't help noticing that no one is punishing you either. And if movement does become possible the only direction is up.

At the bottom of the pit I felt real for the first time in my life, or as long as I could remember. This was my reality: the reality of the shadows, of the dark places. I had tried unsuccessfully to live in the light like my parents, and ignore the darkness that I sensed all around. All my energies had been consumed in that vain effort. Now suddenly I was in the dark; it wrapped around me like a cloak; almost solid, comforting. In the dark everything looked different, softer, harsh edges blurred. And for the first time in my life I was not afraid.

I wrote a poem:

> I have come down the stairs.
> From the top it looked dark
> and I was frightened.
> Now I am here at the bottom
> there is nothing to fear.
> There is nothing.
> And who can fear nothing?

In this place nothing moves. Everything has stopped. The see-saw balances. The pendulum rests. But it is not the kind of balance that precedes action or is a prelude to growth. It is a part of no living cycle. It is not death but it is like death.

It is the opposite of life, that which I feared to fall into. Now I have fallen and the worst is known.

It is not what I expected at all. It is both worse and better. I am here in the mud with the dirt and the detritus, all the waste matter that sinks to the bottom. I am in it, I am part of it. It has its own kind of beauty, harsh and bare. And it is peaceful. There are no demands.

At that time I was fascinated by the outcasts who congregate in the corners of the city: the down and outs, the winos, the homeless. I felt an affinity with them that I could not feel for respectable people going about their respectable business; between them and me there was a wall of glass. I could see them but I could not hear what they were saying, and I couldn't talk to them. That was all right. I had nothing to say to them. I didn't belong, I never had belonged, I didn't want to belong. I could stop pretending. I had always felt an outsider, alone even in a crowd.

I was anchorless, rootless. I was not living, I was not dying, though I knew that if I stayed here too long I might. Life can't be stopped and resumed at will. I had not chosen this place, it had chosen me. For a long time I had fought against it and all knowledge of it. Now I was here. For how long? For ever maybe. I didn't know and I didn't care. Life had been tried and found wanting. If that was all, hard work, loneliness, misery and despair, then I didn't want it.

Part II

'There is no peace, no certainty,
There is no quiet but the solid earth –
The times are normal'

Michael Roberts

i

I was lying on the settee in the front room in a post-migraine limbo: weak but purged, relaxed, almost comatose, in the state of euphoria induced by the end of a day's vomiting. Outside it was a grey, nondescript day. Across the road I could see the trees on the common: oaks and plane trees. It was midday. As I looked they disappeared and were replaced by dark green firs and pine trees, their pointed triangular crowns massing against a deep-blue, cloudless sky. A bright star shone above the trees. It hung shimmering in the centre of the sky radiating a fulgent light on the dark wood below. I gazed open-mouthed, spellbound, incredulous.

Pulling myself up out of my trance I said aloud, 'Well come on then. If we're going to have a bloody revelation let's have it.'

Nothing happened, but slowly the sky lightened and the star faded and gradually the whole scene disappeared and I was looking once more at oaks and plane trees through which not one scrap of sky was visible. I felt very disappointed; wanting to say, you shouldn't take me so seriously I didn't mean it, come back; wishing I'd waited and not been so churlish.

But in the days to come it remained in my thoughts, strange and inexplicable and wondrous, a small miracle. And in the routine of my prosaic days and my depression a secret comfort. I told no one (except Dr P). I didn't want it scoffed at or explained.

*

I sipped my coffee and looked out of the window at the trees on the common, hoping that its scalding heat would dissolve this numbness, the feeling as if my blood had stopped circulating, that had been there since I woke and realised that today was the day. I'd been waiting six months, begun to think I was forgotten. It was as bad as waiting to go into hospital. If I carried on like this the whole thing would be a waste of time. Hospital doctors may only be interested in bodies, but this Dr Penny would expect a little more from me. I was supposed to go in there and emote, tell her my troubles. What troubles? If I don't make an effort I shall miss the bloody appointment. Well that would end it. Not sure I could summon enough energy to make another – even if she would. Still there's plenty of time. Too much. But I don't know how long the journey will take. Two buses – double the delays. Of course by tube it would only take half an hour. But I can't manage that. The mouth of the underground station gapes at me like the entrance to Hades. The last time I was down there I felt suffocated. I couldn't breathe. I had to get out.

I looked round the pleasant sitting-room and tried to relax. Sunbeams were streaking in through the dusty windows bathing the room in sunshine.

The first time I sat here we had just had our offer for the house accepted and I'd come to take some measurements. Then it had been an autumnal sun and the room was bare except for the chair I sat on. I'd looked at the room, furnishing it in my mind. We didn't have much furniture. It was a big jump from the three-roomed flat we'd lived in since we married to a four-bedroomed semi. I had looked at the trees then and been happy. I had always wanted to live here, as near to the country as you could get in London.

Now all would be well. Nick and I would get on better if we weren't stumbling over each other and the children at every turn. We would all have room to expand and some privacy. The children could have a room each. This was what we needed. No one could be happy huddled together as we had been. But they didn't seem to appreciate the space. Looking forward to the first morning in my new kitchen I came downstairs to find them all round the kitchen sink arguing as usual about who should have the first wash. Nick, who'd been brought up in a house without a bathroom, was as bad as the children. There was too much space. The first night the children dragged their mattresses into our bedroom complaining that they couldn't sleep, there were too many strange noises: owls hooting and cows dragging their feet through rustling leaves made me nervous too.

In time we did expand to fill the house and privacy became a necessity again.

I loved that house and the common. We picknicked under the trees. The cat played jungles in the long grass and got scolded for catching birds. The dog, a corgi, embarrassed us by rounding up all the cows that by ancient law are at liberty to graze on common land and startled a horse with her barking into unseating its rider. We had to keep her on a lead, otherwise temptation was too much for her self-control. But I could safely leave the children to play and climb trees in her company. In the early summer I left the front door open and the heady scent of may filled the house, reaching me where I sat sewing in the back room.

Now seven years later all that hope had gone. Nothing had changed. Euphoria had got lost in routine. Nick was more busy and more withdrawn. I was increasingly unhappy, and I'd run out of excuses.

Gathering together my failing willpower I grabbed my hand-bag and made for the door.

*

So far I have talked as if this journey concerned only myself.

In one sense it did: no one else could make it for me. Neither could I make it alone, though I believed that I was meant to. Life that should have expanded with greater knowledge and experience had narrowed until there was no area to it, no time of day that was not a battle against depression and fear. I had to force myself out of the house to go shopping. Beyond the corner of the road where the noise of the High Street assaulted my ears I was seized by panic. When I needed a new outfit for the mayor's annual ball my friend Sarah had to go to the shops with me.

I sat all day smoking 'just another cigarette' until half an hour before the children were due home. Only then did I jerk into a frenzy of activity, tidying up and preparing the tea.

Later I stopped doing even that.

When the fear and the tension became unmanageable I had to get help. I had tried everything I knew; I read books, I learned to relax; nothing made any difference. I was in unknown territory without a map. On the advice of a social worker I went into analysis.

I am much too early, so early that everyone is out at lunch and I stand looking at the large front door, my mind a blank. I have nerved myself, aimed myself towards this place, this moment. It hadn't occurred to me that it might be shut. Finally the one person who is lunching in takes pity on me, or is sufficiently irritated by my repeated ringing to answer the door. She suggests that I come back nearer the time of my appointment. How sensible. Why didn't I think of that? Because I'm afraid that if I go away I won't be able to come back. She gives me permission. She is kind, small, precise, immaculate, and doesn't draw attention to my stupidity, but I'm relieved to discover that she is not Dr Penny. The latter when I finally get to see her is comfortingly nearer my own size, and casual. A vision of colour in a swirling blue skirt, she seems to bounce into the waiting-room radiating health and vitality. I am drab in neutral colours. A thin stick of misery. I fall in love with her immediately.

I can see it, though not in detail; we moved from there later. But I remember the waiting-room and the other customers: some looked ill, some remote and withdrawn, one or two were friendly and chatty – nobody actually looked crazy. I was always the last to be picked up; I arrived early and she was always late, so I had a good view of the other two analysts: one small and nervous – I wouldn't trust him to get me to Oxford Circus – the other large and severe – terrifying, rather like my Aunt Maria. Mine is best. She is at once ideal and unattainable, out of my class. What am I doing here?

Of the words we spoke I recall few: of mine because they had little meaning, of hers because she spoke little; she was always very quiet, laconic.

'Would you like to tell me what has brought you here?' She sits back and folds her arms comfortably. There is all the time in the world. I have told her explicitly in the letter I wrote. What else is there to say? I repeat it, my words sounding ever more foolish. I should have something more important, more dramatic to tell than this dull saga of fear and inability: that I, a Londoner, am unable to travel on the tube, to go farther than the end of the street without panic.

The only question she asks is about my age. After a long and painful pause, in which I wait for her to tell me politely to go away and stop wasting her time, she says, 'Yes, you do need help.' I let my breath out in a long sigh; I seem to have been holding it ever since I arrived. She thinks she can help me! Finally she asks how I would have felt if she had said no. 'Desolate.' She looks a little surprised. I have not shown so much emotion. But it is the exact truth. What would I do? Where else in the world would I go if she sent me away? She is my last chance.

So it was with Dr Penny's support that I was able to let go of some of the rigidity that was holding me together, allow the cracks to widen and the hidden depression to emerge; and with her empathic encouragement face the abyss and not be too afraid to stay there. I could experience the rightness of being there and acknowledge the truth, that I was no longer satisfied with my life as it had been. It was a way of stopping the world for a while. And so real that it comes back in memory as an actual experience, which to me it was.

When she asked what I wanted to do I could only reply, 'Nothing.'

'Perhaps that is what you want, to do nothing,' she said.

Put like that it became a legitimate aim, not just a cause for guilt. I remember the feeling of relief her words gave me.

I sat with my feet in the dirt, my back against the hard rock. Overhead I could see their feet, those busy commuters scurrying to work. It was like the view from a basement. A lot of the time I was one of them. In their world I did only what I had to do to get by. When I could I retreated to the silence at the bottom of the pit, retreating from the world, its busyness, its noise and the necessity to communicate. Here was peace: non-effort, non-involvement. It was bare and stripped of inessentials. Here for the first time for a long time I felt real.

More than anything I wanted to die; every lurch of a bus, every shudder of a train made my heart leap with anticipation. Death would mean the end of pain, the end of striving.

I had tried to make myself into a better person. But I had failed in that as in everything. Dr Penny said I didn't want to die, I wanted to live differently.

At the bottom of the pit with its lack of clutter things looked very different. It began to seem more important to try to be myself, whatever that might mean.

I didn't understand what had happened to me, why I was not content. By most standards mine was a good life. But I was so tense that my bones ached and my stomach was clenched in a knot; sometimes I could hardly walk. When I lay down at night my heart raced and thumped and a pulse beat in my head. When I did sleep I had nightmares, the same one in different forms. I was watching a murder, unable to stop it: I couldn't move, couldn't cry out or make a sound. Awake or asleep I was frightened.

If Dr P was right there were some feelings behind all this. I didn't know what that meant, but I had to trust that she did. I had no feelings. I wanted only to be free of the fear and the unpleasant sensations in my body.

I walk down the street past tall imposing buildings, offices and apartments that were once the homes of affluent city merchants, the world of the rich. It intimidates me. I prepare my first sentence. It hardly matters what. I must say something to kill the silence.

In the silence, tension swells and fills the room like a balloon stretched too taut, that will burst and spill a thousand tiny fragments of me all over the carpet. I am cut off from her by the silence and the tension. Keep talking. Gradually I relax. She says hardly anything; it seems impossible to shock or surprise her.

'I don't know why I'm like this. I don't seem able to get myself out of it. There's nothing to stop me now. When the children were small, and my husband was out a lot . . . but now they're old enough to be left. Of course he's still out a lot. Sometimes it's midnight before he gets home. My daughter had a lot of illness, so she needed a lot of attention. No, well he wasn't there much, and he wasn't very good with them when he was. So I didn't get any help really.'

'How did you feel about that?'

'Feel? Well he works very hard, and it's important work. It's not as if he's just gadding about. And when he is home he still has a lot of work to do . . .'

I waited in vain for her to explain to me what it was all about, and tell me what to do. In months her only comment was, 'Your headaches are the anger with your husband that you can't express.'

I was convinced that she knew, but she wasn't going to tell me. It was like school. You had to find out the answer for yourself. If you get it wrong, go to the bottom of the class. But she didn't laugh or call me silly or say I was making a fuss about nothing. And now and then unexpectedly a remark or a question opened up new vistas.

'I feel so alone. As if nobody cares about me. Though I know they do. But why should they? It's my own fault.'
   'Should I care?'
   'Yes.' I can't lift my eyes above the hem of her skirt. She pays close attention to every word I say, as if what I am saying is of the utmost importance.
   Sometimes she shocks me. 'Where am I in all this?' or, 'Is that how I see you?'
   'No – I don't know – of course not – I hadn't thought about it.'
   What does it have to do with her? Self-centred cow. Why should she be involved? I don't say that. I'm too polite – or cowardly. I can't talk to her so directly. But I can't see that my lowly existence can possibly matter to her. I'm just a problem to be solved, a mistake to be rectified, put on the right track again and passed along the assembly line.
   And she notices things. 'You never take your coat off.' It is a boiling hot day. 'I feel the cold,' I say feebly. How can I tell her that I'm ashamed of my shabby clothes: my skirt that needs pressing, my stockings with runs in, and my ungainly bones? And worst of all, that I'm afraid that my coat may be pinched. As if anyone in that high-class establishment would want it. She makes me aware of myself, unable to ignore the way I feel about myself. And although I don't know that I told her so, it becomes an aim to be able to take my coat

off, and a small victory when I leave it hanging outside in the hall. Nobody stole it!

It took a year or so for the worst of the symptoms to subside, and the streets to feel safe enough for me to walk in. Pavements stayed firm beneath my feet; buildings would not topple, nor unseen assassins menace. The surface of things had become manageable again.

I saw Dr P's job simply as a matter of removing my symptoms, like an operation that would help me function properly. I waited anxiously for her to tell me that our work was finished. Nothing, I thought, could be done for what else ailed me. The only cure for laziness and lack of moral fibre is the time-honoured one of 'pulling yourself together': a cure inhibited by the nature of the problem.

When she said there was more to be done I didn't understand. But I knew that this was the most important thing that had ever happened to me. She was my lifeline; I clung to her like a drowning woman.

I had to let go of the inhibitions and taboos of a lifetime. What held me together and enabled me to present an acceptable face to the world was also killing me: a straitjacket inside which I was dying. I had to let go and trust that she could keep me afloat in the sea of chaos and confusion I would otherwise drown in.

From then on it was rather like riding a bike down a steep hill when your brakes aren't working.

I understood, first of all with my head, that I had suppressed or forgotten certain areas of my experience because they were too painful to remember or not allowed, or maybe both. And in the process I had lost touch with a lot of feelings that I needed. I had been taught to deny negative thoughts and feelings, and, as I learned now, in trying to lose some of them I had lost them all. It's not possible to select. I had also understood that the body was a vehicle to be looked after like any useful piece of machinery. Being was cerebral: the mind controlled the body. But my body didn't agree. Feelings that I had suppressed were expressing themselves through the pain in my body that only began to lessen as I acknowledged the feelings as mine, and allowed my body its due importance.

The energy returned slowly. At first everything was an effort. Dr P said, 'You are sitting on your feelings. That is using all your energy and is why it's so difficult for you to move out of your chair.'

Nick says it's all her fault. She's turned me against him. He knew how it would be. He didn't want me to go into analysis in the first place: a lot of mumbo-jumbo-pseudo-psychological nonsense – like witchcraft. Filling my head up with jargon. If I was bored and unhappy why didn't I get a job, a proper one, full time. What was stopping me? We could get someone in to look after the house, and the children were old enough to look after themselves. True.

This was a familiar argument. He was forgetting conveniently that the last time I worked I ended up in hospital spitting blood and the doctor had said I must not work. In fact each time I started to work I became ill and had to stop. The relief I felt when Dr Taylor said that made me begin to realize that something was wrong. I didn't want to work at all. Nick was a workaholic, so that was his solution to every problem. But his final argument: 'I love you, you love me, it'll be all right as long as we love each other', was the one that always defeated me. I wanted so much for it to be true.

In a way he was right – about Dr P that is. Without her I doubt if I would have had the courage to leave – or even to know that I wanted to. Talking to her revealed the truth that my symptoms were hiding. When I began to think about breaking up with Nick and ending my marriage, my fears of more global destruction left me. But far from encouraging me she was sometimes more understanding of his point of view then I wanted her to be. About what I should do she was usually strictly neutral.

Nick thought I was making a fuss about nothing. Like my parents, his spare time was filled with good works. What was wrong with that? We had a good life. My friend Sarah said, 'You don't know when you're well off. He doesn't drink, he doesn't go with other women, he doesn't beat you. I should be so lucky. A real beg-your-pardon. You want your head examined.' That was the general view. Mine too.

Sarah, her husband and her one year-old son lived upstairs in the house where we lived when we were first married. Now she had the iron staircase to negotiate and we had direct access to the garden. Jessica and Lottie could run in and out.

Sarah and I became good friends after a sticky period in which she thought I was a stuck-up 'beg-your-pardon' and I expected her to be a typical 'Jewish' mother. She paid only lip-service to the strict observance her husband demanded, and kept her bacon in my fridge. I listened to her stories about her awful mother-in-law who even turned back the eiderdown and examined the bedclothes each time she visited. In her turn Sarah was my comfort and distraction when depression threatened, with the kettle always on the boil. She was very good at counting my blessings for me. Her husband was an unsuccessful businessman, gentle and self-deprecating, no competitor. Sarah had grown up in the East End, one of six children of Russian immigrants. She knew all about hardship and hard graft. By comparison I had it easy. She could never understand why I was not satisfied with my life. 'You're a *meshuggene*,' she would say shaking her head. 'Crazy.'

Sometimes you can't win — not if you're a woman — or a woman as I was then. It must be easier, I used to think, well simpler, to be a man: your life divided neatly into two separate worlds, work and home. But as a woman 'lucky' enough to have a husband and children I spent a lot of time trying to please different sets of people, and ended up pleasing no one. When I stayed at home to look after the children, professional acquaintances said, what a pity to waste all that training – and the meaner-minded added, that I as a tax payer have paid for. Teacher friends told me how lucky I was not to have to work. (Where does it come from, the idea that looking after children – unless you get paid for it, of course – is not work?) Headteachers told me how short-staffed they were and what a difference my presence in their school would make. When in response to their pleas, our parlous financial state and my own restlessness and guilt I went back to work, my non-professional friends, of whom there were more then than now (only a few women continued to work after they were married), told me how lucky I was to be able to earn some money and to have something interesting to do, while murmuring about latchkey kids and how the children of working mothers lose out. This might not have mattered so much if I had not been such an easy target. But their words, all of their words simply swelled the burden on my already overladen conscience.

I'm forgetting too the husband who always encouraged me to go out to work (being a progressive thinker and liking the extra money), but somehow didn't expect this to make much difference to his daily routine.

But in one thing I'm afraid my critics were only too correct: I don't think I did a good job in either place. At school I worried about Jessica and Lottie, if they needed me, if they were ill. At home I worried about neglecting my work. At least when I stopped work the guilt was more single-minded. Nick used to ask me what I did all day when I'd omitted to take his suit to the cleaners or mend his socks. The answer should have been, 'worry'.

The solution for a guilt-tripper like me was in voluntary work, political and charitable, fund-raising: jumble sales, bazaars, bring-and-buy and flag days. Boring but unquestionably worthy. Small wonder that I dreamed I was dying at a jumble sale. But no one could criticise or accuse me of wasting my time. Standing on a windy corner with a red nose and numb fingers rattling a collecting box at indifferent passers-by is sufficiently unpleasant to silence all accusers (even me). Sorting out second-hand and sometimes dirty clothes, hiding my revulsion at and my dislike of the rapacious and needy who surged in, over us and out like a cloud of smelly locusts also earned me gold stars in the virtue stakes. In time I came to hate it all. But I was as trapped on the merry-go-round of it as I was in my marriage. I couldn't just leave it to those who did enjoy it, though there were plenty of them. Not even when I was in such a state that I had to walk down the middle of the road to avoid the buildings falling on me and the paving stones splitting under foot.

Above all no one must know. Most of my energy went into trying to appear normal – whatever that is. And succeeding so well that when I admitted that I had to take tranquillizers no one believed me. I didn't manage to extricate myself until I had been seeing Dr P for over a year and had accumulated enough 'good reasons': having to go out to work and to look after Mother who was ill. One of the good reasons, needing to spend more time with Dr P, couldn't be mentioned. Nobody except my family and closest friends knew about her. I was ashamed of my need. Neurosis or self-indulgence – and most of my friends put it in the latter category – neither was acceptable. I concocted elaborate alibis in case I should meet anyone I knew on my way to see her.

ii

Before new trees can grow old wood has to be cleared out of the way. Sometimes old buildings must be demolished before the new can rise in the same place.

First there has to be a death.

A dream: I am at the library with the children who are much younger. We have gone there to hide, from a man I think. We are looking out of a window at a scene that is being enacted on the other side of the road: I am kneeling in the gutter, blood pouring from a severing wound in my neck. The murderer is standing over me with an axe in his hand saying that he is sorry and telling the crowd gathering around us that he didn't mean to do it. Dying I cry out, 'You're sorry. I'm dead.' I tell the children not to be frightened, this is only a dream.

But I was dead. Waking from the dream in which I had died at a jumble sale I looked in the mirror and saw that there was no one there. My eyes were as blank as a switched-off television screen. I have died but no one notices. I was dead and no one knew. As in the dream I continue to walk around as if nothing had happened.

*

According to popular belief everyone remembers where they were when President Kennedy was assassinated. I certainly do. But for me the significance of events was reversed. The Kennedy tragedy orchestrated and provided backcloth for my own particular drama.

November 22nd. 1963. I was sitting in the dining-room watching the president's motorcade on TV. We called it the dining-room but only used it for special occasions: Christmas, the children's birthday parties. It was a gloomy room. We preferred to eat in the cheerful kitchen with its white painted walls, cherry-red wooden chairs and red and grey vinyl floor covering, and its open fireplace. But I had recently moved the TV from the front room to the dining-room. With two growing children and a husband addicted to football and cricket and most other sport the TV was rarely

52

silent. Now an effort had to be made, not a great one, but a definite movement in order to watch TV, and the sitting-room could revert to its more traditional function as a place for reading, for listening to music and even for conversation.

I had the feeling that I was hiding, sitting out here in the back room out of sight of a casual caller. The TV was on, but purely for distraction. My mind wasn't on it. I was waiting for Nick to come home and in my head replaying our conversation of a few nights ago: for us a reasonable, or at least a subdued conversation – no screaming – which somehow made it more deadly – no possibility of reconciliation after such a polite and indifferent exchange. Indifferent on my side, on Nick's more like despair.

'I bore you, don't I?'

I said nothing. It was true, but sounded worse put into words. But he wouldn't let it alone.

'That's what you felt the other night wasn't it – bored?'

'Yes, if you must know.'

It had been a disaster, a pointless exercise. Nick had invited me out for an evening: a meal and a few drinks. A ceasefire, to show me that away from the constant bickering and worse which had become our sole means of communication we could still have a pleasant time together. I knew it wouldn't work, but rather than be accused of not even trying I had gone along with it. So Nick in his best charcoal suit with the faint grey stripe and I in my midnight-blue twopiece with a straight skirt and a subdued floral overprint had spent an uncomfortable evening being polite to each other. I was mostly silent. There were few topics that would not lead us straight into the anger that simmered just under the surface ready to break out at the slightest provocation.

I suppose it had served one purpose: Nick had to admit what I already knew, that the situation between us was hopeless. For me the time for mending marriages was long past. I only wanted to be finished with it. It was true, I was no longer trying. For once he spoke to me without either shouting or pleading: 'You don't love me, do you?'

'No I don't.'

'You never did.'

'That's not true. I did. But I don't now. Not any more.'

'Then there's no point in us staying together.'

'No.' At last something we could agree on.

It seemed obvious that Lottie and I should stay in the house – and Jessica still needed somewhere to come back to at weekends. Nick had been looking for accommodation ever since, without success he said. I wasn't sure that I believed he was really looking.

The unbelievable things that were suddenly taking place in front of me jerked me out of my absorption. I sat watching, tears pouring down my cheeks as they played and replayed the same few moments of tragedy, hoping as I suppose most people were that it would turn out to be a mistake, that the president would somehow survive.

I wasn't sure what or whom I was crying for. Something was ending; a life was ending, a piece of history; my marriage was ending. You could never go back again. Things would never be the same. I cried for all endings.

When Nick came home I was still sitting in front of the TV. He stood in the doorway. He obviously hadn't heard the news, and at that moment I wasn't even thinking about it. Something about him looked different: he was in a hurry, he was still wearing his overcoat and he was seething with barely held-in anger.

He spoke as if he had been rehearsing or was just continuing our conversation: 'I'm not going. You can't make me.'

'But we agreed. What do you mean, not going?'

'I've seen Frank Haskill. He's a lawyer. One of the men at school told me about him. He says I'd be stupid to go. If I go I hand over possession of the house to you. It's my house. If someone's got to go, you go. I'm not going.'

He looked at me triumphantly. I was seized by a spasm of fury, and then suddenly I was ice-cool and clear-headed: no more shilly-shallying. I knew what had been going on. Man to man stuff: put your foot down, old boy, she doesn't mean it. She'll sing a different tune if she sees that you've got the upper hand. She can't turn you out of your own house. Call her bluff. As if, lawyer-like, the whole thing was about a piece of property. I felt very weary.

That was another reason for my anger. We had bought the house with my savings. I had found it in the local paper while he was on one of his excursions abroad: as a language teacher he needed to refresh his knowledge periodically. By the time he returned the sale only awaited his approval. He had concluded the transactions and put the house in his name. I had expected it to be a joint ownership and was upset. He assured me that it meant nothing; the house was ours.

'What's mine is yours. You know that.' He had paid the mortgage. I had put all my earnings into our joint account. But suddenly it was his alone.

Legally he was right. He was right too about who wanted to go: I was leaving him, whoever made the actual move.

I said with precise emphasis, 'Very well then. If you won't go, I will.'

I felt a sudden sharp pain in my left hand. All the while I had been automatically filing my nails. When I looked down I saw that I had filed my thumbnail right down to the quick.

What I had said was true: we had been very much in love. But I sometimes wondered if I had married him simply to have somewhere comfortable to make love; the great out-doors with its hard stony earth and bushes with prickly leaves that snag your clothes and ladder your stockings loses its charm after a while. Warmth and a comfortable bed are more enticing. Sex before marriage, although widely prac-tised among my acquaintance – and judging by the number of girls who 'had to get married' we were not alone, was not openly admitted. Society was more hypocritical then. Girls who 'got themselves into trouble', i.e. pregnant, were widely condemned. I didn't agree with these double standards, but lacked the courage to flout them openly.

iii

Twenty-five years earlier I had stood outside the door of the German professor's room plucking up the courage to knock. Dr Strong: before I met him I had heard that he was a fiend: sarcastic and brutal and a Nazi sympathiser. In the year before the war that was permissible, though not to me. Later he toned down the expression of his more extreme opinions. Our relationship was doomed from the start. Glowing reports from my school had given him a false idea of my competence. 'I understand you are very good,' he said.

I wasn't just the best German student at school, I was the only one. I had passed my written exams well, but opportunities for German conversation had been nil, and German conversation was expected naturally. As usual when faced with an unsolvable problem I fell into a paralysed silence. A disclaimer would only sound like false modesty. He misconstrued my silence as dumb insolence, and stiff-necked pride would not allow me to put him right. It was better to be seen as wilful than stupid. That I became regrettably vocal when he began to expound his admiration for all things German only confirmed his opinion of me as typically English, empty-headed and degenerate: more interested in having a good time than in hard work. The latter was true enough. I had been good for eighteen years. The freedom from my kind, good parents went to my head.

Before I could knock the door in front of me opened revealing a picture of male sophistication (to my eyes): an older man – at least twenty-one, a trilby set at a rakish angle, a college scarf slung carelessly around his shoulders. Thin featured, delicate, fair-complexioned, not my type. I preferred them dark and brooding. With what I took to be an unpleasantly superior smile he said, 'You're new, aren't you? Don't be nervous.'

As I was doing my best to appear calm and confident his words did not reassure me; I thought he was sneering at me.

'You've met Clark? My best student: hard-working and dedicated. I hope you will follow his example.' Dr Strong looked at me sternly over his rimless half-glasses. Clark, I decided, was probably very conceited.

That was my first meeting with Nick. He had already completed his degree and was at the beginning of his teacher training.

I know it must have rained during my time at university. But I don't remember it. I remember extremes: weeks of hot, sunny weather, indolent weather, acquiring a dark gypsy-like tan; or deep-packed snow and slip-sliding all the way down the hill into college. But nothing prosaically in between.

I used to watch out of the train window returning on the first day of term for the colour of the earth to change. I had heard that Devonshire earth was red but assumed that must be an exaggeration. Miraculously it was true, and for me at that unmarked border a different world began. I always tried to pinpoint the exact place where ordinary brown earth became richly red, but however hard I concentrated I always missed it, aware suddenly that the change had occurred without my noticing.

It was a part of the metamorphosis that took place in me every time, beginning as I boarded the train at Paddington with a mixture of relief and guilt. The guilt didn't last long. I don't know if it is like that for everyone in wartime. I had the feeling that life had stopped on Sunday, 3 September at eleven a.m. and would only resume its expected tenor when the war was over. It had not ended but was put on hold for the duration. In the meantime it would be like this: dreary and cold and colourless, to be endured only: living with fear and uncertainty and the ugliness of sudden random injury and death. Not that that was anything to complain about. It was worse for those who were doing the fighting. Nor were there any complaints from my parents, whose faces showed the constant strain of their anxiety for their son, as did the faces of all who had children at the front, or anywhere at the sharp end of danger.

I remember standing at my bedroom window with my mother one night when we were waiting for the war to begin. We were looking towards the glow that was always London at night – later to be seen in flames and clouds of smoke. I was trying to imagine the unimaginable, wondering what war would be like. Mother spoke the only words of self-pity that I ever heard her utter. 'We went through the last war. We've been fighting ever since to make sure it wouldn't happen again. I don't think I can go through it again. I don't think I can stand it.' But of course like everyone else she did. It was the same for everyone, and for once it was, rich and poor alike, though the only bolt hole for the poor was the underground station. Even in suffering there is inequality.

My brother had joined the Medical Corps. Like myself and our parents he believed in non-violence, in pacifism, in the futility of war. It was a difficult time; worse for him, his decision having far-reaching consequences. In the end he decided that he had to be a part of whatever the whole community was going through, as did we all finally. I put up the most resistance. I could never see war as a solution to anything. We had never been close, but I felt closer to him at that time than any other. He did talk to me a little about his dilemma. Joining up solved the immediate problem of what to do with his life. But it was a brutal solution. Six years abroad, always at the bloodiest end of the fighting – with the wounded. When he came back he was a stranger.

That was where my guilt lay. I was escaping. It was a sidestep to a different place, a different time. The war was not irrelevant but somewhere else. We were affected by it; there was a shortage of men and of food and blackout restrictions were the same everywhere. But the lack of street-lighting is felt much less in the country than in town. Perched on the hillside surrounded by fields and woods, although only fifteen minutes' walk from the centre of the city – to a Londoner this was the countryside.

The life of the university went on in its own solipsistic fashion with its own rituals and backward-looking traditions. The Socialist Society was banned so we changed its name to the Freethinkers and our numbers swelled from six to twenty-four for a while. The *Daily Worker* was banned so we all bought it. This was before the USSR became our ally. Women students had to wear long-sleeved blouses, gowns were obligatory at lectures, women were only allowed to wear trousers for the purpose of fencing. My friends and I joined the fencing club. And we all changed for dinner in the evening. I remember cocktails in the warden's sitting-room, trying to make conversation with a bishop's wife. The subject was roses about which I knew nothing. We took it in turns to dine at High Table, a chore universally loathed.

Our greatest excitement came when we elected as president of the students' guild a pacifist and conscientious objector. The principal informed us that we had to choose someone else. We had chosen him because he was very likeable and very popular. It was not a political choice in any way. But it became a question of principle, of democratic freedom: our right to choose and our right to believe as we wanted to, which was what we thought we were fighting for.

The principal called in the police. They lined the walls of the gymnasium where we held our meeting. Everyone came. It was both a relief and a disappointment that everybody was so well behaved, including the police. We took another vote and made the same choice, and informed the principal that we would continue to do so however often we voted. Then we all went home. We heard no more. The principal knew when he was beaten. He was probably thankful to get away so lightly. But in whatever we did I think there was an unspoken recognition among us that the important things were happening elsewhere. Our potty little contretemps was of no significance. This was not the time for the barricades. A part of me was sorry.

I saw Nick occasionally in a group of male friends, all graduates; all sophisticated. How did I know that? They looked bored and gently amused, as if they were contemplating the rest of us from a great height.

There was always a tension between us, a consciousness of each other, a meeting of eyes and looking away, a surreptitious eyeing up and down.

But I continued to dismiss him from my thoughts, associating him always with his mentor, Dr Strong, who had become my *bête noir*. Our dislike was mutual. I could do nothing to please him and very quickly stopped trying. He really believed that woman's place was with the *Kinder, Kirche, und Kurchen*.

The beginning of my second year was the beginning of the war. The men students who had so far outnumbered the women were disappearing in droves: called up or volunteering. I was at a loose end. No longer a fresher, feeling myself to be quite sophisticated now. My boyfriend had gone down and out of my life for ever. I was more conscious of the gap he left in my social life than in my affections.

I had a passion for ballroom dancing and needed a partner. I joined the row of designated 'wallflowers' that lined the big hall where we held our twice weekly hops. Our overbright animation deceived no one as we waited for one of the embarrassed young men lounging by the door to pluck us from our floral isolation. And I walked home alone, passing more slowly-moving or sometimes stationary couples with a nonchalance that was hard to maintain. One of the entwined couples that I passed was Nick and a drama student. I was mortified when he referred to it next morning over coffee and chocolate biscuits in the caff.

'I was sorry to see you all alone last night.'

'No need to be nasty,' I said. 'We can't all be so popular.'

'I wasn't being nasty, I meant I wished I could have been with you.'

I was half mollified, half disbelieving. 'Don't flatter yourself.'

I loved to dance. Once on the floor my inhibitions were forgotten, absorbed in the movement, the union of music and rhythm.

I had suffered much in the past from partners with two left feet. The hunt was on for a man who could dance and hopefully be good company. I wasn't looking for love. In my newly acquired cynicism I didn't believe in it. It was too painful anyway.

Surprisingly, Nick was said to be a very good dancer. His nickname among his cronies was Dancer. The story was that he had crashed a townee ball and won a prize for dancing. He was drunk and remembered nothing the next morning. But there was the silver tray as evidence.

Academic men are (or were then) rarely good at dancing. on the whole they despised it as a non-cerebral activity. But the dance hall was the best place for getting acquainted with a girl without too much of a commitment. Nick, at popular request, was holding a dancing class. I joined. I didn't need lessons. But I had decided that he would be my new partner.

He was a beautiful dancer. On the dance floor we fitted perfectly, my long legs matching his. If only we could have gone on dancing.

But inevitably the sexual attraction that had made us aware of each other took over, and subdued my antagonism. Now I discovered another Nick: shy and sensitive; an idealist who intended to write a book that would convert ordinary people to Socialism. Not superior, not a snob. How I had misjudged him. A spell in the sickroom with flu, during which time I missed him abominably, convinced me. I was in love. Long before the snow had cleared from the hills and the thawing ice had come tumbling down the gutters we were lovers – in every sense except the final consummation, for which it was much too cold.

I have always suffered intensely in the cold and remember clearly the bitter cold of that first winter of the war, remember numb fingers and feet I could hardly walk on, but remember too how completely I disregarded them in the vast emptiness of our starry-eyed winter universe.

The puritanical attitude of the authorities – men were only allowed into the women's hostels for Sunday tea in the common-room from three to six p.m. – meant that serious 'necking' had to take place out of doors, in whatever shelter could be found.

We walked up the hill until we could see the whole town spread out below. On a wooden seat in the lee of a stone wall we huddled together. Nick wrapped my feet in his college scarf. The fields fell steeply away, the world was literally at our feet. In the moonlight, snow-covered roofs were dark-edged, trees hidden under their burden indistinguishable, vague irregular humps outlined in black and white: a gleaming, silent world. A fairytale place from a picture engraved by Arthur Rackham. It was an enchanted time always cut short. We had to be in by ten-thirty. Even five minutes late and the worst was assumed. Immoral behaviour – and what else could be going on at that time of night – was punished, if you were a woman, by being sent down. The men were more likely to be fined. Ten shillings was the going rate. It was safer to stay out really late until everybody who cared about our morals was likely to be asleep. Fortunately I was never caught. The ground-floor windows were nailed shut. But the back door was always left open for me by my friend and room-mate Dorothy, for whom I did the same. In the summer it was easier. We stayed out all night.

Nick and I were fortunate. During the war male graduates were allowed extra privileges. They were all waiting to be called up. It was hardly appropriate to treat them like children. They were allowed visitors every evening, provided they kept to the public rooms. The wives and children of RAF officers were billeted on their hall of residence, adding an atmosphere of informality and providing us with camouflage. The RAF wives were very friendly and sympathetic, always ready to vouch for me as their visitor if I were seen coming from Nick's room.

Every evening after dinner we rolled back the carpet in the common-room and danced: *Blue Moon, Begin the Beguine, The Breeze and I*; slow and sensual, the same records again and again. With the lights turned low we danced and danced; as one without thought or care. No one disturbed us.

On the radio recently someone remarked that everyone has a time in their life that is their happiest time, their 'blue remembered hills.' I don't know if that is true for everyone but I have no difficulty in naming mine: it was those three years at university. Surprisingly I even knew at the time how happy I was. I remember the particular day.

I was standing under a tree in the Rougemont Gardens waiting for Nick who was coming down for the Whit ball. It was a brilliant June day in my final year: blue sky, warm sunshine, and a gentle breeze just as ordered. I had passed all my exams by the narrowest of margins, confounding my critics, who had confidently predicted failure. At that moment I had no worries. I was content.

Nick was late. I stood under the tree's dense shade – it was a cedar with beautifully spreading branches – dazzled by the brilliant display of colour, savouring the moment, self-contained and still with happiness; my happiness made all the more sweet by the knowledge that it could not last.

There was a war on, as everyone was always needlessly

reminding everyone else. I would soon be going back to London and the bombs, to the devastated streets, nightly air-raid warnings, worried, anxious faces, people who would confide their sad stories to me while waiting for a bus. I would be taking up the serious business of life, beginning a career I was almost certain I didn't want. It was the end of an idyll.

*

During the war, life was speeded up by the knowledge of its uncertainty. *Carpe diem* – seize the day – there may not be another. That is always so but we don't live as if it is. Only in wartime is death so constantly and immediately present and this moment the only one we can feel sure of. There is a pressure then to take what life offers; tomorrow we may be dead.

It's useless to speculate on what might have been. Six years. Those were the years when I was supposed to be growing up – though I see no signs that I did. When the war began I was barely out of school, when it ended I had a husband and a child. Neither had been a part of my immediate plan, though both were included at some vague later date. I was aware even then that I had a lot of growing up to do.

Back home from college, life was very different: living at home, my social life nil. Former friends were nearly all dispersed by the war. Dorothy and I had intended to share a flat. But she was working in rural Hertfordshire and I could not leave my silently unhappy mother who was making herself ill doing voluntary work while my father spent his nights on air-raid duty in the docks.

I was right about one thing. I did not like teaching. I liked children individually but not *en masse*. They needed a degree of attention I didn't want to give and I hated the discipline, the feeling that I myself was back at school, doing what I was told, not what I wanted to be doing.

I became an air-raid warden. And, surrounded by men none of whom raised a flutter in my breast, discovered the truth of the popular song: 'They're either too young or too old . . .' The youngest, the chief warden, was nearly forty – pretty old. But I enjoyed it: the camaraderie of long wakeful nights; life stories shared in the enforced intimacy of hot cocoa and cigarettes in the small pasteboard box that was our office; sleeping on a camp-bed fully dressed, woken at five a.m., my hair in curlers, to a steaming hot mug of tea, returning home to wash and change for school. Though we had no bombs in our area during my time, there was a feeling of doing our bit, of being in a very small way part of the war effort – manning the barricades at last!

A tuberculous violinist with a hollow chest and the long tapering fingers of an artist, a retired gardener with arthritis, a middle-aged clerk and a housewife who spent all her time knitting and being bravely terrified would not have qualified even for the Home Guard. The chief warden and I were the only ones who were fit. He had a severely handicapped child which kept him out of the army, and I was in a reserved occupation. If heroic deeds were done by air-raid wardens, as I'm sure they were, it was not by one of us. I remember the moment of sheer terror as the booming guns woke me, often before the air-raid siren had sounded, tumbling out of bed and running all the way to HQ – a tin hut on a piece of waste land five minutes away; emerging a little later to patrol the streets with a colleague, sauntering, telling others to take shelter, feeling absurdly safe in my dark blue uniform and my official position, protected only by my tin hat. Searchlights swept the sky, gunfire flickered; we watched dogfights: two tiny planes pinpointed by the crisscrossing lights swooped and swerved until one spiralled downwards trailing smoke. If ours won we cheered. It was as unreal as a video game.

Pieces of shrapnel, jagged-edged and dangerous, clattered on to the pavement reminding us that it was not a game.

I can't gauge the effect of the war on Nick. He wanted to be a flyer, a pilot in the RAF. But he was graded 4F, unfit for active service, and allowed to continue teaching. He had stomach ulcers. With no uniform or visible handicap he was a target for the ignorant and the stupid. 'Why should my boy be fighting for the likes of you?' Women shouted insults after us. I was the one who responded. I know he felt humiliated. But all he said, mocking himself, was, 'And what did you do in the war, Daddy?' On crowded trains soldiers made way and found a seat for me and Jessica but roughly shouldered Nick out of the way. White feathers were no longer handed out but condemnation was just as swift and as thoughtless.

It is in peacetime that we really discover the futility of war. War is not expected to be anything but awful. It may be heroic, even exciting if you like danger, but it is peace we long for and talk about with nostalgia. I have never understood those for whom, from the tales they endlessly retell, the war was apparently the 'best of times'.

Peace is our shining goal, our deliverance, our paradise. And inevitably therefore it disappoints. It is not as we expected; though the fighting is ended there are still the same deprivations and the same difficulties to contend with. It is not peaceful. Without the bond of common purpose, like children without a guiding parent we fall to quarrelling. We have forgotten what ordinary life is like. Now the enemy is vanquished we have no scapegoat; we have no one to blame but each other. For all our brave talk about a new world the old rules still apply.

Jessica and I were toiling slowly up the hill towards the railway station. The war was over; no need to feel guilty about exposing her to danger, no need to hurry home. It was a luxurious feeling.

Coming towards us I saw Miss Anstey, a fellow air-raid warden. Now we could have a pleasant chat: admiration for Jessica, who was very charming, and cosy reminiscences. I smiled remembering enamel tea mugs which she obviously found distasteful and the thawing of her reserve as we both put our hair in curlers ready for the night and covered them with a headscarf, turban-fashion.

As we came abreast she looked straight through me and walked on.

*

By the time I was thirty I felt that life was over. Not in years – it might go on for a long time yet – but like a barometer that was set permanently at No Change.

On my birthday, I thought, this is your life: your family, your friends, your worthwhile projects to keep you busy. Why did the prospect dismay me? There was nothing wrong with the life. Only I was inadequate, lazy and restless. Those dreams I'd had, so vague and unreal, must be finally relinquished: 'childish things' to be put away yet again. I didn't know how to mould life as I wanted it, didn't think I should even try. It was I who must change.

At a meeting of our local discussion group – it had been started during the war when political meetings were banned – the chief medical officer, a charming Scottish woman, scolded me roundly. I was bemoaning the boredom of domestic life in the company of two small children whose vocabulary contained no words of more than two syllables. (There were no pre-school playgroups then.)

'You young women make me cross. You don't know how lucky you are. You have a husband. You have children. How many women whose men were killed in the war would give their eye teeth to be in your shoes.' Who could argue with that? Her fiancé had been killed in the Great War. Now once again there were many women in a similar position.

My mother-in-law said, 'Now you've coom to your cake and milk. 'ow do you like it?' She didn't believe in education for girls. 'A waste of time. You don't need a degree to look after babbies.'

I didn't like it. I wished I did.

Mother said, 'Now that Nick's on the council you really must smarten yourself up. You want to be a credit to him, don't you? I'll help you choose a couple of nice dresses.'

She was right of course.

I looked forward to the mayor's ball. I felt good in my new ballerina length plain dark purple, my first evening dress for years. But Nick had lost interest in dancing. Few of the local dignitaries danced; a quick shuffle round the floor to please the wife and a retreat to the bar for most of the evening where more weighty matters − it was implied − would be discussed. The wives for the most part sat around the edge of the hall and chatted: 'That's men for you. Who needs 'em?' Sometimes they danced together.

I refused to join them and accompanied Nick to the bar, the only viable alternative, as did several other young wives, but my feet itched to be dancing.

The food was always good. The children looked forward to the goodies we brought back: *petits fours* and marzipan fruits.

Nick didn't talk easily about himself or his feelings.

'I'm a simple man,' he would say if I tried to talk about mine. 'You're too deep for me. I love you, you know that. That's all that matters.'

If things were going his way he was happy. If not he lost his temper, made a fuss, calmed down and apologized − and everything was as before. He worked very hard and regarded home as the place where he came back to unwind. I used to tell him that he needed two wives: one motherly and domesticated to keep hearth and home together, to wait up with hot food and warm slippers, and one intelligent and attractive to take about and be proud of on social occasions. Unfortunately I wasn't either of them. I loved my children but hated domesticity. I liked a few friends around but was too shy to enjoy public gatherings. I was slow to anger and slow to recover from it. I forgave but did not easily forget.

I don't know whether such differences matter much if you love someone enough. I didn't love him enough. That was the disservice I did him.

He dealt with problems, personal ones that is, by ignoring them. On behalf of those he represented he was indefatigable. He became more and more immersed in work and public affairs. We saw little of each other except at weekends when we did things with the children. Alone together – which we rarely were – we had nothing much to say. I was bored, disenchanted and lonely.

'Aren't you ever going to sleep with me again?'

I had intended to be casual, neutrally enquiring. But I sounded plaintive, hurt. I looked across to the other bed at my apparently sleeping husband. It happened every night lately, the too quick transition from reading to the even breathing of sleep, allowing no space for communication.

We had had separate beds since Nick's slipped disc had necessitated his sleeping with a board under his mattress.

He turned and looked at me, half smiling, humouring me.

'I wouldn't say not ever. But at our age . . .' He shrugged.

'At our age what?' Having got his attention I was not letting go until I'd got something clear. He would have to spell it out.

'It's well known that desire lessens when you get to our age.'

He was forty. I was thirty-seven.

'Not to me. It hasn't happened to me. It's part of being married. We might as well not be if we don't have sex.'

'I didn't say we never would. Just that it's not so important. We have finer things in our relationship.'

I was silenced.

'Goodnight. I really am tired. I love you.' He was soon genuinely asleep.

But I sat wide-eyed until it grew light, transfixed by the question I could hear echoing in my head: 'What finer things?'

At some time in the night Nick half-woke and saw me still sitting bolt upright.

'What are you doing? Can't you sleep?'

'Hammering nails in a coffin,' I said coldly. But my melodrama had no effect, he was asleep again. I was relieved. I didn't want a confrontation. I was too shocked myself by what I was looking at. Melodrama felt appropriate.

What finer things? I couldn't think of any.

Sex was the thing that held us together. Without it we were as far apart as mere aquaintances.

We never had sex again. Nick made a few desultory attempts, but his heart wasn't in it. By that time mine wasn't either. Once the idea had sunk in my desire did lessen. He was prophetically right about that.

That was when it began, the end of our marriage, though I didn't admit it for several years.

I had intended to wait until the children left home. But once I knew how I felt events gathered their own momentum. Jessica had already gone, in a travesty of a daughter growing up and leaving home, telling us that she couldn't bear to go on living under the same roof with our constant rows; and her father's final words apostrophizing her as a 'rat leaving the sinking ship' echoing in her ears.

Within two weeks of telling Nick that I was determined to leave I had found myself and Lottie a large bedsitting room with two beds, a slice of a kitchen and a shared bathroom and was away. It was in a leafy street two minutes from Lottie's school and fifteen from my parents, one stop up on the underground.

Shocked friends assured Nick I would soon be back. He

had not been able to take me seriously until I told him I was actually going. He wanted to believe them. But what they none of them understood — how should they? — was that I was merely making a reality of something that for me had happened a long, long time ago. Like a plant that has been alternately overwatered and neglected (and from the beginning was probably too sickly to survive), we had maintained the outer appearance of our marriage while within the vital essence withered and died.

But I digress. For the moment I am still at the bottom of the pit dismantling my life: the faulty jerry-built construction I had made of it.

Nick was a part of but by no means the whole source of my unhappiness. That was built into my relationship not only with him but the whole world. At the time I blamed it all on him: his neglect, his selfishness, his volatile temper and general inability to see anyone else's point of view. I had to hate him in order to leave him. It was the only way I could combat my dreadful tendency towards self-immolation. The trouble was that we both expected of each other nothing less than the completion of our selves, compensation for every inadequacy and the resolution of all problems. For which I took too much responsibility and he too little.

iii

Now my marriage is over and for the first time I am alone. Now I find myself in this place which seems to be where I am meant to be, where I belong. Here I am at home, myself an outcast. In every other place I feel alien.

In the ordinary, everyday world that I inhabited people who were married stayed married, grew old together. I have cut myself adrift from that world, and its stability.

It has arrived, the crunch, inevitable, unavoidable. Impasse: as the dictionary says, a position from which there is no escape. No husband, no home, no job, no money – no hope.

I tell her that I'm running out of money and will shortly be unable to pay her.

'So you think your husband and I should support you.'

I say icily, 'I don't want anyone to support me. I will pay you as long as I can, and then I will stop coming.'

My cheeks burn. I am humiliated. I wrap the tattered remnants of my dignity around myself, but it's no use. She has taken everything away, everything I thought good about myself, my good temper, my pleasant manner, my helpfulness, my self-deprecation, that now turns out to be just another form of vanity and self-serving. Now she takes my pride.

There is a long silence. Finally she says gently, 'I will charge you a pound a time until you find a job.' I am at once filled with relief – she's not going to send me away – and even more humiliated. She must despise me. I despise myself. I can't wait to get out of the room. I want to run and hide. At last she rises and leads the way to the door. She puts out her hand to turn the doorknob. It turns and turns and goes on turning uselessly. We are locked in. She looks at me and grins mischievously. Wounded feelings forgotten I smile back. Magically the door opens and I go on my way laughing, reprieved. She doesn't hate me after all. Life goes on.

Now I have Mrs Rainbow, my landlady, whose sole topic of conversation is her husband's health. Occasionally it's her children, but only when she wants me to babysit. Mr Rainbow suffers from headaches. Mr Rainbow works very hard and gets very tired. Mr Rainbow needs his sleep. Which means that we have to creep around like mice. No sound at all is permitted after ten p.m. when Mr Rainbow goes to bed. Any infringement brings Mrs R scurrying upstairs. We live on the first floor directly above them. We have no doorbell of our own.

Mrs Rainbow answers the door and vets every caller and turns them away if she doesn't approve of them. Those are usually certain of Lottie's boyfriends whom she finds too scruffy or too familiar. It's hardest on Lottie and her friends. Mrs R makes no allowance for youthful high spirits. I am too depressed and too easily cowed to object. Also it's not easy to find cheap accommodation in a pleasant neighbourhood, which this is. Mr R, encountered in the hall, wears a pleasant and slightly apologetic smile. On the rare occasions when his wife goes out he is friendly and quite chatty, but I think her style of management suits him on the whole. It makes life easier − for him.

I share the bathroom with a woman who doesn't seem to have a regular job and delights in taking long leisurely baths just when I'm getting ready for work, ignoring all my exhortations. It's very difficult when the only lavatory is also in the bathroom. This anti-social behaviour is explained one evening when I hear her being evicted by both Rainbows together. They are finding it as difficult to get rid of her as I do to get her out of the bathroom. It is the outrage in Mrs Rainbow's voice that enlightens me: '. . . not having your sort in our house . . .' Miss X is a prostitute. I had noticed that she liked to sit by her open window in the evening, but made nothing of it.

This is not the respectable suburbia I am used to. This is the obverse side of the coin. I am not surprised, though nevertheless indignant, when walking on the green at the end of the road in the evening, to be accosted by more than one bowler-hatted and rolled-umbrella-ed gent on his way home from business. I seem to have lost the aura of respectability that used to protect me from such behaviour. Or is it more simply that I didn't loiter on the green after dark when I was married, having other things to do? I feel like one of the 'raggle taggle gipsies-o'. This is what you get for leaving your 'truly wedded lord'.

Lottie and I take it in turn to use our room. It is plenty large enough for two, but icy in winter with a one-bar electric fire eating up money. Lottie naturally wants time alone with her boyfriend and I don't want to see anyone. I have given no-one my address but my father. Mother is dying, but slowly.

When they are out I sit looking down the hill where the street lights stretch out like a jewelled necklace. I am alone. For ever. The lights come on as the sky darkens. People everywhere talking, laughing, crying, meeting, parting, cheating, killing. Nothing to do with me. I don't want to be here. I don't want to be anywhere. But here is preferable to where I was before. I don't have to pretend any more to an interest that I don't feel. As the door closes I hear Michael saying, 'Does she ever move?' and Lottie's reply, 'She'll still be sitting there when we come back.' When they are gone the silence closes over me like water rising over my head. I lift my hand, the waters part and close again as it moves and then is still. The silence is complete.

The children return laughing and noisy, shattering the silence and warming me a little with their exuberance.

On the evenings when it is my turn to go out I go to the launderette or walk as far as the golf-course. It is better to have an objective. Lighted rooms before the curtains are drawn fascinate me. Book-lined walls, comfortable chairs, pictures and soft colours: other people's lives inviting and falsely seductive. Old-time dancing in the church hall: Victor Sylvester and strict tempo, the Military Two Step. I long to be in there, but I know I would hate it if I were. 'Won't you change partners and dance with me?' That song used to make me cry when I was eighteen, in my first year at college, and had been jilted. I want someone to swap lives. But who would be daft enough?

It is only to be expected that I am not allowed access to the

Rainbows' phone except in the direst emergency, nor to have one of my own.

Nick has taken to leaving messages with my father that he needs to discuss something with me. As I suspect, these urgent matters are really only excuses to talk to me. We need to discuss money, he says. He gives me a small sum each week for Lottie, for myself nothing. I have no legal right to anything as I have left him. There is nothing to discuss. We must talk about divorce, he says. I can't divorce him and he can't divorce me until more time has elapsed. We both know all this.

Nevertheless I cannot bring myself to ignore his messages. I walk to the underground station late in the evening when it is quiet. The booking clerk gives me change for the phone and suggests I'd be better joining him in his parlour than phoning someone who makes me look so miserable. I feel too low and lacking in self-esteem to respond, but it's nice to be fancied.

Nick's disembodied voice coming over the wire sounds so familiar − 'How are you? How's Lottie? It's been a long time!' − bringing echoes of other calls to tell me where he is and when he'll be home: a familiar routine that is almost hypnotic in its power. What am I doing in this draughty hall, in this lonely place when I could be safe and warm at home? The impulse is strong to say, yes I'm coming home, I'll be home soon. I put the phone down and back away from it as if it is alive. Walking down the road I gather around me the sights and sounds of the night: the wide tree-lined road, the hedges and neat gardens; an orderly agreeable place; the scents of summer drift up from sleeping flower-beds. My feet are solid on the pavement and I know where I'm going and why.

I dream that I am back, in the kitchen preparing supper. Nick reads the evening paper. The children are reading or playing. The cat and the dog drowse in front of a blazing fire. It is so cosy, so right. I want to say, 'But I don't live here any more.' But am stopped by their absolute and tacit acceptance of the situation. A nightmare of normality. I wake sweating and anxious.

Returning from shopping in the High Road, my mind somewhere else, my feet turn automatically down familiar streets. I come to with a jolt, shocked, and turn back towards the bus stop. Sarah says, 'You must really want to go back to him.' She is always trying to devise ways of getting us together. But I do not need the feeling of relief nor the feeling of having had a narrow escape to convince me. I know I will never go back again.

I had begun to do home tuition with sick children before I left Nick, in order to pay for my analysis. He couldn't afford to pay, he said, and I did gain some semblance of independence. But the work isn't regular enough to provide a living. Sick children recover and go back to school or sometimes into hospital.

My father had given me some money so that I could leave Nick. I had none of my own. But that money soon went. So I acquired a succession of additional part-time jobs: in the children's psychiatric ward of a large hospital, teaching reading to groups of children in a primary school and finally in a remedial reading unit. As these jobs succeeded and overlapped one another I wasn't in one place long enough to have to be a part of the staff. That suited me. I was very anti-social and left at the end of each day feeling as if I had escaped.

*

After a year of searching the papers and tramping the pavements I have finally found a self-contained and unfurnished flat: the top floor of a small terraced house. Lottie and I can have a room each. It's cheap and I can have my own furniture. Nick and I have divided things up equally and fairly. Mrs

R says she is sorry I'm going. I smile hypocritically, outside with warmth, inside with malice and relief.

I have escaped from Mrs Rainbow. Now I have my own front door at the top of a narrow staircase and my own bathroom, Lottie has her own bedroom. It's a dull and boring was-once-more-prosperous suburb. Rows of identical little terraced houses in endless mean streets. This was before the shortage of houses has led to a middle-class influx and the tarting up of such places. The only sense of life and colour is in the noisy High Street market with its colourful stalls of cheap gaudy clothes and materials and the wisecracking patter of the stallholders. I can afford to live here. I hate it. But I know no one and no one knows me. So I like it too. Here I am no one: no one's daughter or wife or mother – well I am that, but Lottie has left school so she doesn't want to be reminded of it either. I am trying to make my external world match the way I feel inside: not good, not beautiful, not 'worthwhile'.

Nobody comes here except the children and their friends and Jonah. Nick followed me home one night, he had to know where I was, but I didn't invite him in and he didn't come again. Sundays and Bank holidays are the worst days. Happy families are on parade and the greatest sin is to be alone. If I stay in I feel trapped, with the walls closing in on me. If I go out I am exposed, a visible failure.

Colleagues don't understand how I can bear to live there: 'It's so squalid and depressing.' So am I.

My landlord, Mr Tozer, is small and as tough as the East End he comes from; rather resembling the badly glazed garden gnomes he fills his garden with, and very kind; scolding me when he discovers that I have been ill, making me promise to let him know in the future, clearing the lavatory pipes blocked by my own stupidity with discretion and delicacy, lending me an extra heater when the snow comes in through badly fitting windows, and in summer leaving me tight bunches of flowers from the garden wrapped in silver foil on the stairs. His wife is deaf and their music, Strauss and Mantovani *fortissimo*, conveniently drowns out any noise Lottie and her friends care to make.

*

She turns my world upside down.

'You always have to do what other people want? Why shouldn't you do what you want?'

'Well, it's bound to be wrong.'

'How is that?'

'It always is.'

'So how do you decide what to do?'

'I put my wishes on one side and consider the alternatives, then I choose the best one of those.'

'Why put your wishes on one side?'

'It would be selfish not to – it wouldn't be right.' She looks incredulous, and I say defensively, 'Aren't we supposed to put other people first?'

'Always?'

I can't explain it to her. That's how it is, always has been, always will be. I wouldn't get what I want anyway, so there's no point in wanting it. Those who ask don't get, so Mother always said. That those who don't ask don't get either, I'm beginning to learn.

Another day. 'If a thing's worth doing, it's worth doing well,' I say, quoting Mother.

She grins. 'Have you heard the other saying, that if a thing's worth doing, it's worth doing badly?' I laugh. It's nice to be teased. But there's a sting in the tail. I can't bear to do anything badly, I would rather do nothing – and usually do.

She says, 'How do you learn to do anything if you don't practise? Babies aren't born knowing how to walk.'

Like Brer Rabbit I 'lie low and say nuthin' '. But I have heard what she said. For Christmas I wrote her a poem:

Sometimes it seems hardly feasible
to pay a psychiatrist to prove to me
how unreasonable I am.
to listen to my nonsense as if it matters
somehow shatters my former ideas
and resolves my fears.
I always thought it your job to make people sane.
But you seem to have made me quite mad,
and I'm glad.

She is becoming more and more necessary to me. Between sessions the days of the week sag like an unused washing line.

Depression, the abyss of nothingness, is being filled up with pain: a jagged-edged knife in the guts, lacerating, unbearable. I can tell her about it. But that brings no relief. Does she even believe me? When I'm with her I'm tense and inarticulate, but the pain goes. She makes it disappear. As Mother always did, she makes me feel safe, but I don't expect her to understand. She isn't like Mother but I'm always afraid she will be. Each time I bring her some 'news from the interior' I expect her to scoff. I can't bear this pain. How can she?

But today it doesn't go. It has taken over. I can't move or speak. I am transfixed; like a butterfly pinned to the back of my chair, my hands clutching the armrests, my arms rigid. This seems to go on for a long time. I turn my eyes towards her and see that she is mirroring my position, sitting straight back against her chair, her arms on the armrests, not as if she can't move, but as if she is aware of the intensity of feeling, and that I am locked inside it. She doesn't know how to help me. Can I tell her? I want her to understand how awful it is, and I don't want her to send me away. I dread the end of the session. My voice emerges with difficulty from my locked throat.

'Do you know about the pain?'

'Do I know about your pain?'

'No.' I shake my head. 'Your own.'

She looks at me intently and says simply, 'Yes, I do.'

She isn't going to tell me it's not so bad. She isn't going to say it could be worse. She believes me. She knows what it is like, because she has felt it too. She doesn't have to deny it. She is looking at me in a way I don't understand, as if she is suffering with me – for me. Can that be true? Is this what they call empathy?

Suddenly something seems to let go, to relax, and the pain moves, loosening its grip, spreading out along my arms and legs to my toes and my fingertips, thinning out as it goes, through the rest of my body. I am shaky and weak, as if a fever has abated suddenly. It is some time before I can move. I have lost all sense of time. When I leave I see that I have been there an hour and a half.

It is winter. Even in town the earth has been locked for several weeks under layer upon layer of hard-packed snow. Except on the main roads the ground is iron-hard and very slippery. Trying to walk I am like a fish out of water floundering on the frozen bank: I am afraid to move one foot in front of the other.

A few days later, leaving my parents' house I find the snow has disappeared; there has been a sudden thaw. Walking should be easy, but I find it as hard as if the roads were still icy. I turn into the callbox at the end of the road and ring Dr P.

'I can't move. I don't know what to do.'

She suggests I ring a friend and ask her to come and take me home. When Sarah arrives I burst into tears.

'Oh dear,' she says, 'I thought you were better.'

'Yes I am,' I say, crying and laughing at the same time; laughing because I can ask for help and cry in public and do both without minding; laughing at the paradox of appearing worse when in fact I'm feeling better. Like the weather I have had a sudden thaw. It takes a bit of getting used to. I feel very odd. I think I may have joined the human race.

*

Explanations sound so tidy, as if this caused that and that caused the other in orderly sequence, like a game of Consequences. But it wasn't like that at all.

Moments stand out, moments of recognition, moments of truth, premonitions of change. Moments in what overall felt like some kind of polite hell. I didn't progress, I lurched, I staggered; I fell and doubted I would ever rise again, or that I would care. Progress was a pessimistic one step forward, two back. Miserable and abject I sat and complained, or didn't; and gradually uncovered my pain, my guilt, my sorrow, and much later my anger, in response to the gentle but merciless probing of the quiet woman who sat opposite me. Sitting there like a rock; not demanding yet demanding everything; not giving yet promising everything; from whom I dared ask and expect nothing but from whom I wanted everything; and who gave unstintingly when I was able to ask. Sometimes there was a glimpse, as of the starving come to a feast. Can she eat, will it make her sick, or will it be taken away, will it vanish as everything promised so far has?

There was a dream I had of a beggar dozing in the middle of a hot dusty square, dreaming of a banquet; tables piled high with food. But as he goes eagerly towards the feast he knows he is sick and cannot eat. He wakes in the empty square, flies buzzing round his head and the taste of bile in his throat.

It is difficult to describe how insight and understanding came about. First of all straight from the unconscious in the form of dreams and images: a series of moving pictures that speak more vividly and convincingly than words. They have stayed in my memory when most of the words have gone. It is like a photographic record of my life at different stages; but a record the camera couldn't capture, visible only to the inward eye; a different way of seeing, a different way of knowing.

Dreams were often precursors of change. For instance, awareness of what Winnicott called the false self, which led to the conviction that my whole life had been a sham, a lie, merely a façade behind which I hid my true worthlessness. I had a dream about the death of a king. His treasure chest had been closely guarded during his lifetime. After his death they opened it. It was empty. The soldiers had been guarding nothing. As I already knew. Dr P said I felt such a strong need to protect my treasure that I had hidden it even from myself. I couldn't believe that. But still, she thought I had something worth protecting.

If I was existing by means of a false self, where was my 'true' self – if I possessed such a thing? I doubted it. I saw no evidence.

But then I had another dream. Someone gave me a pig to look after. I didn't want it. But they said it would root around and finds its own food. So I agreed. But one day I found it dying. I tried to give it some milk but I was too late. It keeled over and died. As it did so it turned into a beautiful white bird. I was overcome with remorse for having neglected it and allowed it to die. Dr P asked me whom I had neglected. I could think of no one. 'Myself?' She nodded.

Dreams were the commentaries, like the Greek chorus: highlighting the action, explaining, pointing out dangers and mistakes, giving a voice to my unconscious wishes. Like oracles, not always easy to interpret: often seeming frivolous and irrelevant, or doomladen.

I was haunted by the sound of a child crying. In my mind I saw a shabby little boy with a wistful face standing on a hill somewhere far away.

At my lowest ebb I dreamed of a baby: an amazing baby that grew rapidly, walking and talking at a few months and smiling at me with confidence and joy.

Sometime later a little girl appeared to plague me. I recognised her: myself aged between three and four years. I drew her as she stood with her back to me. I came across the drawing only the other day: short straight brown hair, sturdy body, chubby legs and hands clasped behind her.

She won't turn round. When finally she does she still refuses to talk to me. She just stands there and looks at me reproachfully. I hate that child. Why won't she leave me alone? Why does she look at me like that?

Eventually I persuaded her to hold my hand and finally to sit on my knee, but only after I had said I was sorry and promised to look after her. She took a lot of persuading and I can't say I blame her. She had no reason to trust me, I hadn't treated her well. After that she became a good companion. I talked to her when I was lonely or afraid and we gave each other courage. I kept my promise – more or less. I tried to look after her. But I'm ashamed to say that quite often when she appeared my first words were, 'Oh, go away!'

She still turns up now and then, but only if I'm in danger of forgetting her.

Bits of me that I had forgotten or disowned, that I had become cut off from appeared to me as separate and autonomous beings. They had to be like that for their own protection. So they might not be destroyed again. At a safe distance I could look at them when I was ready and reconsider them. I had to learn to believe that they were mine, that they did and could belong to me. They had got lost in the process of trying to make myself into the sort of person that I thought my mother wanted me to be. I despised all those messy, untidy, unmanageable bits that didn't fit. In the end it was only myself I was fighting.

What do you want? What *you* want? Once said the words won't disappear. They reverberate, sending echoes down long empty tunnels, bouncing off desolate walls, off years of not wanting, of not daring to, of not seeing any point. Now they won't be banished. They come unbidden; always most inconveniently; forcing me through the agonies of having to ask. It's easier to want something I can get for myself. But once let out of its cage this animal is a ravening monster; it won't be told to lie down and go to sleep, or be sensible, not to be silly, not to be greedy. And the thing I want? A photograph of Dr P – to have and to hold – what presumption. She doesn't seem to think so, she will have to look one out. When it doesn't materialise the next week, I am convinced she didn't mean it. Why should she? I am a fool to have let myself look forward to it. I lose my voice and can only croak, can't talk to Jonah or tell him why, feeling intensely foolish. Finally ring her and ask why she didn't bring the photo to the session. 'Oh I forgot,' she says airily as if it is of little consequence. 'No, of course I don't mind. I just haven't got around to it.'

That tiny photograph, just a head and shoulders, has long been lost. But at the time it was the most treasured of my possessions; it sustained me through more than one crisis; the sight of her face enabled me to carry on when I felt I absolutely could not.

From my first-floor window I see her slow approach as she turns the corner, head down, hands in pockets, a fag drooping from her lips, ignoring the steady downpour of rain. Resistance in every inch of her.

'Let me take your coat. You must be soaked.'

'So what? I like walking in the rain. Smoking and walking in the rain – great.'

It's the longest speech she has made so far and the first admission of liking anything. The cigarette has disappeared so we don't have to have an argument about that.

She has run away again and been fetched back by the police. A man she knows has betrayed her by telling them where she had gone.

Carol (she prefers that to Emily, her real name which she despises) is the adolescent embodiment of how I feel but wouldn't dare to behave – exceedingly anti-social. She has been thrown out of every secondary girls' school in the borough, and has reluctantly agreed to come to me for tuition every Saturday morning – but only under threat of being removed from the care of her adoptive mum: the one person she seems to have any affection for.

I have persuaded her mum to let her come for her lessons as usual. 'She ought be punished, naughty girl, causing everyone so much trouble.'

'I'm glad you're back.' She looks defeated and very depressed.

'I'm not. You're just like the rest. I suppose you think I'm a bad girl worrying my mum. Well she's not my mum. And I don't care. You've got no right, nobody has, to stop me doing what I want.'

'It's because I care about what happens to you. Your mum does too. I'm glad your friend told the police where you were.'

'Don't give me that. Why should you care? You're my teacher. It's nothing to you. You do it 'cos you need the money.'

Total scorn and disbelief glared at me from pebble-brown eyes under a long fringe of auburn hair. 'He's a rotten bastard. He promised he wouldn't tell.'

'You don't understand the danger you were in in the West End. It isn't safe for a young girl on her own. And I do care.'

She turned to face me squarely as if to say, let's get this woman sorted out once and for all.

'Why should I believe you? I don't. That's what they all say. Why should it matter to you? Why should you care if I'm in danger?'

Over her shoulder I can see Dr P's photo on the mantelpiece, at this distance quite indistinct. I fix my eyes on it. How can I expect to get anywhere with this girl? No one else has. I do like her. I like her honesty and her reckless courage. But I don't know why she should believe me. I take a deep breath. 'I don't know why you should believe me. It isn't something I can prove. All I can say is that I have a daughter and if she were alone in London I should like to think that someone like your friend would take the trouble too help her.'

'Oh – well.' She's disconcerted and turns away from me looking out of the window, her face expressionless, the dark curtain of her hair coming down to hide her. My heart sinks.

Suddenly she swings round and with a grin that I rarely see says, 'I thought I come 'ere to work. What about them sums then?'

Carol writes poetry and funny stories, learns to type and, with no qualifications but nerve and personality, lands herself a job as secretary to a man running a small business.

'My mum thinks I should be satisfied stacking shelves in Sainsbury's. That's not for me.'

I have let her use my typewriter to practise on, and admitted that I'm learning myself but not doing very well. Her final words to me as she leaves with a grin and a nod towards the typewriter: 'You'd better get practising then.'

iv

Gratitude can be a heavy burden. I felt I had to be grateful to my parents, those hardworking providers, especially my life-saving mother; a debt I couldn't begin to pay. I felt guilty about that. 'Why should you be grateful?' Dr Penny said. 'You aren't even sure that you wanted to be born.' True. If they'd asked me I would have said no. I felt bad about that too. But to be born meant being ill and nearly dying; it meant pain and discomfort; being left in my cot unfed and uncomforted, deserted by my mother, as I saw it. I recovered, that is, I didn't die, and for this I was supposed to be grateful.

For forty years I'd accepted the 'authorised version', the 'aren't you lucky to have such devoted parents' routine. Now

I was looking at things a different way, trying to see how it had been for that baby who grew up to feel unloved and unwanted. What did she know about a mother who agonized over her, who was unable to feed her or stop her pain but who refused to give up hope even when told that her baby was dying? What does a baby know of its mother's feelings? It only knows what it experiences. What do parents know about a baby's feelings? That was the trouble. In our family feelings had little credit. They were meant at all times to be kept under control and measured out like cod-liver oil in appropriate doses. Babies were allowed a certain leeway in this, but not much. Talking about that time Mother said, 'When you recovered from your illness you became very clinging. You couldn't bear to let me out of your sight. But I soon put a stop to that.'

The first time she left me I cried all afternoon until she returned. Neither my father nor my aunt could comfort or distract me.

Mother was a very busy woman, involved in political and social reform. She couldn't allow a whining baby to interfere with her work. I soon learned not to cry.

My parents belonged to the 'child as clay to be moulded' school of thought. So they didn't look to discover how the child was, but rather how they wanted it to be. They expected us, my brother and I, to cooperate in this. And as their methods were on the whole kind and humane we usually did.

Was it the gratitude I resented? Or the conditions it imposed: the obligation to repay, never mentioned but implicit, never demanded, denied even, but nevertheless expected for ever and ever?

I remember my father, when I'd stayed with Nick longer than we'd arranged, 'How can you be so selfish, leaving your mother alone while the air-raids are on? You don't think of anything but your own pleasure.' That was true. We were very much in love. Mother said nothing, looked white and suffered silently – her *forte*. Father also was leaving Mother alone with the air-raids, while he firewatched. That was ok He had a good reason. Everything was ok if you had a good reason. Being in love was not a good reason.

Another time he actually gave the game away. I had just begun to work full time after my marriage ended and was beginning to feel a renewal of vigour; that a new start might be possible. But Mother was seriously ill. He asked me if I would give up some of my work to look after her, and incidentally him. I must have looked as reluctant as I felt. When I didn't immediately respond he said, 'I'd have thought you'd feel it your duty – No, of course I don't mean that. But she has always worked hard and looked after us.' Yes she had. And I did what he asked.

I was still being breastfed when the abrupt and painful separation of my illness occurred. No one knew exactly what happened. My grandmother brushed a large fly away from my mouth when I was lying in my pram in the garden. Perhaps it had deposited some infection. I vomited for a fortnight and was unable to take in any nourishment. That led to intussusception of the bowel. I was too weak to be operated on. Nothing could be done. According to the two separate consultants the doctor called in, I was dying. By some miracle I survived. By my mother's devotion I was told. My mother who never took her clothes off and whose hair went grey overnight.

That it was painful for her too she never acknowledged, so I was left with all the pain and discomfort. How could I understand what she never admitted, that we were both at the mercy of the forces outside our control?

To me she was all powerful. If I suffered pain and she did nothing to stop it, either she wanted me to suffer or I deserved to. That my mother could wantonly inflict pain was unthinkable. I must have deserved it. I never knew exactly what crime I was guilty of. It seemed to concern my very existence. I had no ticket of entry. No entitlement to be here. Cast out of the universe, expelled from the earth I clawed my way back, hanging on by my fingernails, expecting every moment to be discovered and thrown out again. I should have died, but had obstinately refused to.

Waking from a deep sleep I experienced for a second time the heaviness in my blocked bowels and the nausea rising in my throat. I was alone in a dark void with no one and nothing to hold on to, falling endlessly. As I fell I heard a voice that said, 'I hope you die.' Fully awake I found that I was lying curled up on my side like a baby, sucking my fingers. I drew a picture. A baby is lying on a cloud. Out of the heavens a huge hand appears with the index finger pointing straight down. The finger tips the cloud, the baby falls off the cloud and begins its endless descent.

I wasn't always grateful to Dr P either. When Mother died I felt as if part of me had died. There was a raw wound I couldn't bear anyone to touch. That summer was a real heatwave; the grass in Hyde Park was pale brown, burnt tinder-dry. The asphalt bubbled and sizzled on newly mended roads on the way to the hospital. It was situated in the slummiest, poorest part of town. The hard midday sun exposed the bare bones of tawdry poverty, and filtering through high grimy windows delineated the bare bones of age and senility in the whitewashed crowded ward. What right had I to live in a pleasant neighbourhood in relative comfort? That wasn't how I usually described my sparsely furnished bedsit. But today it felt as if I personally were responsible for these ugly, unlovely, undernourished lives, and I alone had condemned my mother to end her days here in a sea of madness and degeneration.

*

For as long as I can remember my parents used to talk about

what they would do when they retired. They planned to move to the country, to a small bungalow with a large garden where Dad could indulge his passion for growing things and Mother could enjoy a return to the sort of place she had grown up in and always missed.

I too looked forward to it. I much preferred the country to the boring suburb we lived in. Who, given a choice, would choose to live among rows of small terraced houses, relieved only by the occasional dirt park whose once grassy lawns had been worn into baldness by the many bicycles, tricycles, scooters, roller skates and boards on wheels that raced around them every evening? Even the bit of forest we impinged on was choked by grey-leaved dust from the trams and the trolleybuses and the trippers who spilled out of them every weekend from the East End of London. Stunted shrubs and trees, and on bank holidays a plentiful crop of newspaper, sweet wrappers, tin cans, lemonade bottles and orange peel.

I innocently assumed that I would be living at the bungalow too. But even when I realised my mistake I still thought it a good idea: it would enable them to stop working so hard for others and enjoy their life together.

The first time they took a holiday without us I was sixteen. They went to Scotland to assist in the setting up of a new Woodcraft group. My brother and I were camping at Lake Coniston. On our last morning they were to arrive at Coniston at eight a.m. from Glasgow. We rowed up the lake to meet them through the gently swirling mists, the prow of the boat making arrows in the milky water.

For the first time in sixteen years I saw my parents as strangers. They stood on the empty dock waiting for us – they had arrived early – both in the green Woodcraft costume: she with a short skirt and a headscarf tied gipsy-fashion, he in a jerkin and corduroy shorts; looking younger than their years, arm-in-arm, relaxed, smiling, ineffably content with the world and with each other. A rare snapshot.

But the bungalow was a pipedream.

Father's retirement coincided with the end of the war. They were both very tired. Mother looked ill but denied it, though she couldn't deny the rheumatism that made her feet and her fingers so painful.

Who would want to buy a war-damaged house in a war-damaged city? There was an acute shortage of houses. Some people were even making permanent homes out of temporary summer accommodation. My father was a cautious man, and by that time had other irons in the fire.

For him retirement brought a new lease of life.

All his working life he had done his boring office job because it was secure and had a pension at the end of it. He was lucky in the depression years to have a job at all.

Life began for him when he came home from work with his voluntary activities, mainly the Woodcraft Folk. But during the war the Woodcraft Folk was banned, as were all so-called political organisations. So Dad began to take a more active part in local affairs – hitherto Mother's domain – and soon joined her on the County Council. At first it was a shared pleasure, departing together for County Hall each day. They both enjoyed the cut and thrust of debate and manoeuvring for power and chewing it over at the end of the day.

Husbands might retire but wives did not. Dad had only himself to get ready, Mother had all the chores to fit into her day. It did not occur to him that she needed extra help and she would not ask. What happened seemed inevitable: he was a man and he was popular: he was given the chair of a committee that had been promised to her. He offered to resign when he saw how it upset her but she wouldn't hear of it.

Mother became depressed and forgetful. The doctor advised her to slow down. She resigned from the council, saying he had told her to. Alone all day in a too-big house she sank into further depression. I called in nearly every day and often found her crying.

'Don't tell your father. It would only upset him.'

So strong are the prohibitions of childhood, it did not occur to me to disobey her until it was already too late.

On a visit to our GP with one of the children I chided him for making her give up the activities she enjoyed. 'I did not,' he replied, 'that was her own doing. But I'm afraid you must realise that this is only the beginning of senile dementia.'

It was another ten years before she died.

Deterioration set in gradually at first, then more rapidly until she was living entirely in her own fantasy world. When she could no longer be left alone Dad gave up his council work to look after her.

'She's always looked after me. Now it's my turn.'

She never knew that I had left Nick and sometimes asked where he was. But mostly she thought I was her favourite younger sister, Edith.

She had moments of lucidity. One day we were standing looking out of the kitchen window. 'Do you see those pigeons on the roof over there? Your father would say I'd imagined them.'

'He thinks I'm a silly old woman,' she told the doctor. 'I suppose you do too. You don't believe me either.'

The doctor said tactfully, 'I do believe that you see the things you tell us about, but unfortunately we don't.'

Coming in from the garden, she said, 'There are some very nice people out there. I had an interesting conversation with a chrysanthemum gentleman.'

I would discover her standing on the back doorstep with her hat on and the shears in her hand, a bewildered look on her face. 'Mother, you can't go out there, it's pouring with rain. Come inside.'

'But I only wanted to cut the hedge.'

When I arrived in the morning she was still in bed.

'I'll be up in a moment. I was telling Mother' – nodding at a photograph on the mantelpiece – 'that I'm not really lazy, but I can't get up while all these people are in the room. Some of the men have brought their bicycles. I think they want to have a meeting.'

I opened the bedroom door and made shooing movements.

'Everybody out. Come along.'

She smiled with relief, 'Oh good, they do as you tell them.'

Dad could not cope with being woken two or three times in the night to see her standing at the window. It overlooked the back garden. There was a multitude of shadows to add to her confusion.

'Come back to bed, Aggie, you'll catch cold.'

'There's a child outside. Can't you hear it crying? It must be cold. Will you fetch it in?'

'It's the wind or a cat. It's nothing to worry about.'

But nothing would convince her or comfort her distress. Finally he would shout in exasperation, 'For God's sake, Aggie, let's get some sleep.' And then feel ashamed at the stricken look on her face.

The strain was telling on my father. His blood pressure was too high. He was nearly eighty years old. His mind could not encompass the idea that his rational, practical wife, his helpmate for fifty years, was lost to him for ever.

The doctor sent Mother into the local hospital to give Dad a rest.

In the crowded geriatric ward the beds were barely fifteen inches apart. The nurses were too busy and too impatient to humour her. There she was only one of many, and quieter than most.

'You tell them,' she said to me. There were hectic red patches on her cheeks and a frantic look in her eyes. 'They'll listen to you. They won't listen to me. I want to lead the women in singing. Stand on that chair.'

She put her hands together as if to clap for silence but could make no sound. The noise of the visiting families did not diminish. And the momentary light in her eyes dulled.

The last time I saw her she was fitfully dozing, her eyes set in dark-bruised hollows, eyelids fluttering, her hands moving restlessly over the bedcovers.

Suddenly her eyes opened and she looked at me quite sanely. Her eyes were pools of weariness. She spoke the comforting words of my childhood, words she only used when some awful disaster had happened that she couldn't make better: 'Never mind.'

And her eyes closed again. She died early next morning, unattended.

V

I could have stayed in the park all day, lying on the grass, letting the sun melt my bones. Why do I bother to come? For this genteel torture? I am never going to be any better. My hopes are buried in the grave with Mother.

A fragment of a poem: 'The blackhearted psychiatrist uses the finest steel to disembowel me.' I never finished it. I didn't know how to. I think I just wanted to be rude to her. It's all right for her, she takes me apart with practised ease. But who's going to put me together again? She doesn't care. Why should she? Anyway I don't want her to. Indifference is a virtue. I've had it with love. (She doesn't seem to care how much I abuse her.)

The summer that Mother died I had to get away.

It had been January when I left Nick and the icy weather reflected the cold polished tidiness of the house I was leaving and the deep chill that had entered into my bones. I felt nothing. Packing the last few garments I said to Lottie, 'I don't even know why I'm leaving.' 'I do,' she said, 'I know.' Mother died in July of the same year. By then the coldness of winter had given way to the heat of summer. But nothing altered or affected the coldness inside me.

The ten years that Mother suffered from senile dementia had been a terrible strain on my father. But he was lost without her. He had never been alone before and never without a woman to look after him. Though that position had been reversed in the last few years.

He clung to me with fierce desperation. He couldn't bear me out of his sight and became very anxious if I was late home. I stayed with him all that summer. But for one week at the end of August I booked myself a caravan on the edge of the Norfolk marshes.

I had never been anywhere by myself for more than a day. I was scared stiff.

I was an alien presence among the happy holidaymakers who crowded the train. In the midst of the noise and the banter I had never felt more alone.

It was a very new campsite with few amenities. A travelling shop arrived and departed early in the morning before I was up. It was a mile to walk to the nearest village.

Behind us a chequered pattern of fields, green and gold and brown, covered the lower slopes of the rising hills, rolling away into the purple distance, crowned with clumps of bushes, fringed with trees – a typically English landscape. Before us a distant blur of blue sky, sun and sea concealed the marshes, invisible in the dazzling heat of an August afternoon. The weather had been and continued to be very hot.

We arrived together, they by car, I by taxi drawing up in the small country lane, and I was glad to follow them across the fields to the campsite. They were a young couple with two children and had been here before. They issued a cordial invitation to join them and fraternise with the regulars in the village pub later in the evening, but I politely declined. 'Perhaps another time.'

A dozen or so new caravans were dotted at well-spaced

intervals around the field. As I looked across the unmown grass from my comfortable oblong box I wondered what I was doing here. The other caravans were all occupied by couples or families, middle class, mostly with young children.

I turned night into day, gazing for hours at the thickly starred sky and the bright harvest moon from the wide window above my bunk bed, as if I would wrest some meaning from them, eventually falling uneasily asleep as daylight approached. At midday as the families of bucket-and-spade-clad children straggled wearily back from the beach I was emerging gingerly from my caravan like an invalid shrinking from the light. In the drowsing afternoon I had the wide expanse of marsh to myself: the subdued grey, green and lavender of tough, scrubby tenacious sea plants, tiny rivulets of clear water winding through parched mudflats to the sea. On the dunes a few battered pines an inadequate windbreak. An occasional sea bird on lazy wings gliding slowly by. The horizon was lost in a pale haze of sun and sea.

I was alone in the world. No life but tiny crabs and little scuttling, slithering boneless colourless creatures. Following a meandering path to the distant sea I was terrified when a sudden mist enfolded me silently and completely. All sense of direction or distance deserted me. I might drown in the rapidly advancing sea.

Just as suddenly a vagrant breeze dispersed the mist and the sea returned to its less threatening place a mile away. And I returned to the safety of the dunes.

In the evening when the moon hung low on the horizon, tired children were fast asleep and those adults who could had departed for the village pub I walked out again and sat on the salt-scrubbed trunk of a fallen tree and experienced a different kind of silence.

The marsh etched in black and silver was more menacing, more mysterious, hiding its face, remote and withdrawn. But the darkness was not frightening. It was impersonal, hiding me too from all the things I couldn't manage. Violence and danger were far away.

With the slow passing of time and daily minutiae closely observed came a feeling of peace and healing. I followed the path across deserted fields, the corn already gathered in, to the village. In the small secluded graveyard of the Gothic church with its gravestones overgrown and half-obliterated, soaking in the sun, I found a sense of life unexpectedly sharp and invigorating, of life continuing independent of me. The creatures in the mud, the scrubby plants, the ragged pines and the birds were alive, as the bodies mouldering in the churchyard once had been. And so was I. I needed no more reason than they. In this desolate and beautiful place that was like a hiatus in time, where everything pleases the eye, there was nothing and no one to interrupt my reverie, and I was at peace. I could contemplate Mother's dying and accept it for what it was: just one event, a pinpoint in the eternally recurring cycle of life and death.

On the last day of my holiday I spoke to my neighbours who had tactfully ignored me all week. They said they thought I looked unhappy, as if I wanted to be left alone. I told them my mother had died and gave them my leftover food.

Back in London the heat is unbearable. Petrol and exhaust fumes dance in a deathly shimmering haze above the pavement. Too many bodies jostle. In the park there is some small relief, and now and then a stray breath of air stirs the languid trees. Jonah has just walked away. He's had enough, he says: I won't talk, I won't do anything. Well, I can lie there all day and play silly buggers and get sunburnt if I want to. He doesn't have to.

He stays for a while under the trees. I can see him out of the corner of my eye. He expects me to come after him. Usually I do. But not today. I would like him to stay but I can't say so. Why should he when I can't even tell him what's the matter? I don't know what he sees in me. He knows I'm lost. I never notice where we're going. I just follow where he goes. But today it doesn't matter. Nothing matters, that's the problem. And I can't explain it to him.

There has to be a limit to his patience. He puts up with my moods mostly (as I do his). If he doesn't we have a row and that brings me to life. But today he can't provoke me. I know I've gone too far. The next time I look he has gone. It's a relief. I want to be lost. I'm not fit company. I press my bones hard into the dry grass. I would like to disappear, not to exist. I can't even cry. I don't want to move. But finally I have to. I can't stay here all day. My father is waiting. And that's the problem too. I sit up and begin to brush the dead grass off my skirt. I don't know the way to the station. I shall have to ask someone. I begin to panic. Then I remember that it doesn't matter.

Jonah is coming across the grass carrying two ice-cream cones. He says, 'I knew you wouldn't be able to find your way home without me.'

*

The climb out of the abyss was slow, with many setbacks. There was never any point at which I could say, I've arrived. It was more like scaling one peak after another to discover yet another always beyond. The best that can be said for the climb is that it toughens the muscles and the view from the top is wonderful.

Dr P said once, much later on when I could take such remarks with more equanimity: 'You have everything the wrong way round.'

It was as if all my photographs were printed as negatives, so that I saw everything in reverse: black as white, light as dark. I had spent all my life trying to work out what other people wanted, keeping my own wants hidden even from myself. She turned the searchlight on me. Like a moth caught in its beam I wriggled in an agony of exposure. She was not concerned with right or wrong, with what ought or should be. She wanted to know how I felt, what I wanted, what I needed. I expected philosophy, theory, jargon, words of wisdom: areas I was woefully lacking in. Instead I got: 'But what do you *want*?'

'What do you mean?' (Behind every question I suspect hidden criticism.)

'What I say.'

'But how do I know? When? Now?'

'Yes, why not?'

Must be a catch in it. But I can't alter her words or make them sound any different. Immediately, what I want is to go to the lavatory. What a relief! I don't have to sit on it till the end of the session as I usually do, and then bolt for the nearest public toilet. But such a trivial thing to want. Why can't I want something worthwhile? She looks pleased.

That's how it went; not in great flashes of light or roads to Damascus; no eurekas – just small, unimportant, hard-won, amazing steps. To some only a lavatory, to me Mecca.

Dr P has to go into hospital, for a minor op, she says. I'm thrown into utter panic. She may die.

'Don't go, don't leave me,' I long to say – but don't. 'What will I do without you?'

That she should cease to be is not possible, is not bearable: the unbearable that has to be borne. I work hard to avoid it, but it sneaks up on me when least expected.

But in the midst of all the misery, all the confusion and uncertainty something has been quietly growing. It is like walking through an endless desert and without warning coming upon a tree; not a mirage, just a tree growing as if it is an ordinary thing to do in the midst of dryness and emptiness; as when it rains and the desert suddenly bursts into blossom. Only the fear of losing you makes me lift my head from my self-absorption long enough to look and see what you have come to mean to me. Not just a time slotted into the week for the convenient evacuation of all my shit, not just a lifebelt to hold on to.

Before you went into hospital I gave you a poem I had written:

> You grow and flower in me like a tree.
> That is love, tender, unfolding green leaves.
> And you are mine to love.
> You may go elsewhere and still be mine.
> I will curl myself around you gently,
> protecting, and hold you still in me.
> I may lose you harshly, painfully.
> But I have known you for a while,
> perhaps for ever.

I give you the poem before we finish, hoping to escape before you read it. It feels presumptuous; you have others to love and protect you. But you remain obstinately in your chair and take your time, reading slowly. I am already standing by the door. I have just been telling you, though I know I shouldn't, that I am nothing and have nothing when you're not there.

'Isn't this something you can have?'

'I don't know.'

I want to say no, how can it be? But I lack the courage.

Against all the evidence, that is contrary to my expectations, you didn't die. You came back.

In my first glimpse of her Dr P was like the fairy off the top of the christmas tree: pink and white and sparkling. In our sessions she was quiet and gentle. In my dreams she was a severe but benign headmistress exhorting me to do better, or a social worker come to inspect my house. In later dreams she was my comfort, showing me the way when I was lost. And finally my lover. That was startling and confusing, reflecting nothing of our sessions where I usually sat stiff and self-contained and inarticulate.

It is painful to be in love with one's analyst, it being necessarily a one-sided exercise. But on the other hand in no other instance of unrequited love is so much wholehearted expression of feeling not only allowed but positively encouraged. And much as I longed for it I would have been terrified if she had reciprocated. As she knew better than I, it was a mother I wanted not a lover. But in the reawakening of homosexual feeling it is not always possible to tell the difference.

It is hard to become a child again. But it had to happen. She became the whole world to me, my first love as my mother had been.

Reparation and reconciliation was not possible with my parents. They could not have understood what I found them guilty of. They had done their best. Nor could I face them with it. I wasn't sure I had any right to. If at all it had to take place within myself – but not by myself.

To one brought up to believe in moderation and balance, *mens sana in corpore sano*, one step over the limit is a step towards total demoralization. Mother would never stay in bed past nine a.m. however badly she had slept. 'It doesn't do to give in. You never know where it will end.' In utter sloth and degeneration obviously. The lesson was so well learned that I have difficulty staying in bed even when I'm ill.

Giving way to my emotions, as Dr P encouraged me to, was like opening the floodgates of a dam. I was knocked sideways by a flood of unfamiliar sensations. I was exhausted, I felt ill. The first time I lost my temper I lost my voice. My emotional muscles were rusty, lacking exercise.

All my life I had believed that anger was not only dangerous but unnecessary (as well as making you feel very uncomfortable). It achieved nothing. There was always a better way to get things done.

It was the same with fear. 'There is nothing to be feared

but fear itself.' Franklyn Roosevelt said that. I used to admire him. He was of the same generation as my parents. It was Dr P who showed me that fear is a necessary warning of danger. Otherwise we should be like the small boy I knew who launched himself confidently from the highest step whether Daddy was there to catch him or not. He ended up with a cracked skull.

Mother rejected any display of emotion, especially in public, as vulgar and shallow. 'Real feelings, deep feelings are private. People who make a parade of them are just showing off. You know your father and I love you, we don't have to keep telling you.' I had just been telling her about a little girl I went to school with whose mother hugged and kissed her every morning and waved her goodbye from the front gate. I don't remember her name, but I disliked her and thought she and her mother were very silly.

Habits become more fixed as we grow older. I reacted to excess of feeling like a hypnotised rabbit. From my father I learned to pass things off with a joke, to ease my embarrassment. Coming home late at night through empty streets I was convinced a man was following me. I could hear his feet on the pavement behind me. He had a knife in his hand poised to strike. I was paralysed with fear. Nick had to meet me if I was out after dark. He was very good about it. Of course it was silly of me. Frightened of a shadow!

Dr P said, 'You can't deal with things by pretending they're not there.'

Mother used to say, quoting her own mother, 'Let not the sun go down upon thy wrath.' But really it wouldn't have surfaced at all if she'd had her way.

I have begun to move around the room. It is very important that she stay where she is. I have this image of a toddler just learning to walk, staggering away from Mummy on unsteady feet, a little way – a bit further – and still further, but always hurrying back to Mummy.

The first time it happened I was quite unprepared.

'The sun is shining in my eyes and making my head ache.' I thought she would offer to change places. But not at all.

'I like sitting here,' she said firmly. She had her back to the sun. 'So what can you do?'

Me? So far, only what she gives me permission to do, preferably in triplicate. I feel peeved. But she looks unrepentant. (Mother would have told me what to do, she wouldn't have let me flounder.)

'Well I suppose – I mean I could – could I – I mean could I move my chair?' Oh dear. The only possible place is occupied by a plant. This is beyond me. I can't even begin. She takes pity on me.

'I'll move the plant while you move the chair.'

The whole thing is accomplished in a mad dash. Afterwards we laugh and there is a feeling of great daring and novelty: the idea that I can alter something if I don't like it.

In time I become a most intrepid traveller: from chair to couch and back again. I sit, I lie, I stand. And look back with pity on that poor feeble worm who couldn't lift her eyes above the hem of a skirt.

(Many ages later I sit on the floor beside her, my back to the radiator, not the most comfortable of positions but my favourite; to be so close that I can feel every movement and hear her breathe and occasionally lean against her and cry.)

*

I'm ambling up the road at my usual depressed speed. What is there to hurry for? All I want now is a cup of coffee. She passes me like a steam train at full throttle.

'Just hurrying to do some shopping,' she tosses over her shoulder. It's getting near Christmas.

She needn't worry. I wouldn't expect her to stop and

chat. What does one say to one's analyst by way of polite conversation? 'How's your psyche?'? She knows too well how mine is. Anyway I'm not sure I would have recognized her if she hadn't spoken; she looks like any suburban house-wife, with her headscarf and her shopping bag. A bird of paradise, a bird of prey – in a headscarf?

It is strange this box I keep her in, and my inordinate fear, as well as Pandora-like longing, of letting her escape. Sometimes I see her on the underground train as we both make our way towards our appointment. I have conquered my claustrophobic fear of crowds and enclosed spaces. When this happens, I shut my eyes, ostrich-like, and pretend she's not there. I never mention these meetings, nor does she, so I have no idea if she sees me. I can never decide what is so terrifying about seeing her out there. Is it something to do with all the despicable things she knows about me? Is she going to tell everybody: 'That woman never makes her bed. She told me so herself'?

I am convinced that she wouldn't like to see me either, and would be particularly annoyed to find me trespassing on what feels like her territory.

The entryphone crackles: 'Hallo.' The voice is young, female, with a certain likeness but definitely not hers. I panic, check my watch and the day.

'I have an appointment with Dr Penny.'

'Oh? What time?'

'Er – now?' – apologetically.

'Ah. Late as usual.'

That has to be a daughter: the slight tone of disparagement combined with good-humoured acceptance.

'Can you make your own way in? Do you know where to go?' Friendly and casual. Panic eases.

'Yes. Thank you.'

'Dr P works from home now. It is more convenient and cheaper.

It's hard to believe that I have been doing this for seven years, two or three times a week. No one, not even I, questions it now. It has become just as much a part of me as brushing my teeth, doing the washing or the weekly shopping. I have survived.

To me the move is both exciting and terrifying: so many pitfalls and lurking dangers. At the Society all the public areas were communal, mine as much as anyone's. Not that I believed that, but intellectually I knew it. I had a right to be there. Here I feel as if I'm following a narrow path through a swamp. If I stray who knows what perils may lie behind those impassively closed doors? I have a right only in two places: the waiting room and the consulting room. I scurry nervously, or feel as if I do, between one and the other, with occasional forays to the bathroom.

As I remember it was late summer when we moved. Our new room is on the second floor. So much light: chimneys and treetops and sky. I can breathe up here. I love to look out of the window, measure the seasons by the changing trees, follow the clouds and the birds as they chase across the sky.

It is strange: in my memory the other room was always dark. It was on the ground floor in the angle of the building. Net curtains kept most of the light out. But that suited me then: I didn't want to see or be seen.

The doors all tend to look the same, painted the same anonymous cream. The second week of the new regime I choose the wrong one. It is a broom cupboard.

'Next one along,' she says calmly.

The idea of stumbling into her private domain horrifies me. I apologize. But have to admit, though not at that stage to her, it also intrigues me.

She says she can't make up her mind about closed doors and anonymity, so sometimes they're shut, sometimes not. A sly peek through an open door is as shockingly exciting to me as a glimpse of ankle to an earlier generation. The kitchen: orange, or is it tangerine? – she likes bright colours.

The sitting room: comfortable and pleasant but not smart. I avert my eyes and hug the details to myself to be mulled over later. It's a secret. When I tell her, as I usually do in the end, she says I'm a little girl who wants to explore and find out what Mummy gets up to when she's not around. I'm ashamed of that, but she makes it sound all right. Inside the room it's more difficult. This is her furniture, these are her pictures on the wall. It is nothing like my fantasy – much more low key and ordinary: two deep armchairs, a plain divan for the couch – that's all. There's nothing to dislike except the carpet – a sickly green – and that was already down. She didn't choose it. But the room has an unfinished look. I can suspend judgement. By the time it is finished it has become just the place where we work and play and have our being: our room.

I am in fact obsessed with everything about her, and although I still find it difficult to look at her directly, I know every detail of her appearance, and cherish the opportunities for secret observation. I watch her approach from the doorstep where I'm sitting waiting for her. She swings along at a leisurely stride; no hurry, not phased if she's late, looking comfortable in her body, her face in neutral, relaxing into a half smile and a friendly glint as she sees me. I knew her car would be red!

Once again it is high summer. Emotion blossoms in the heat of the sun. The hot dusty pavement scorches my sandalled feet as I walk from the station down the back streets, through the square to her house. The few people that are about move slowly. Midday heat has driven even the tourists inside.

Coming towards me a young woman in a full cotton skirt, a palette of brilliant colours, concentrating all the intensity of the sun. She looks frowning and anxious. When I am a few feet from her I say, 'What a lovely skirt.' Her face clears and she smiles with relief, 'Oh thank you.' I hadn't realised that I was staring. My friendliness takes me by surprise as much as it does her.

I am so in love with her (Dr P that is). I learn Schubert's *Serenade* by heart – fortunately I can't sing. But I quote: ' "I will build me a willow cabin at your gate, and halloo your name to the reverberate hills." '

Sometimes I meet 'Daddy' on the stairs when I have an early appointment. We exchange a stilted good morning. Yes. Tall, fair, attractive. Not quite as artistic as I expected but he will do. My fantasies run riot.

After meeting him the willow cabin becomes a workman's hut on the pavement, where I sit and brew endless cups of tea and inveigle 'hubby' in for a chat and a gossip and a chance to complain about 'the wife'. Why can my imagination not stay on a more exalted plane?

The door-buzzer sounds mid-session.

It is a cold drizzly day in February. I am quite at home here now. Thank God she feels the cold as I do. The gas fire as well as the central heating creates a nice warm fug.

We both jump. She answers politely at first, then more coldly, 'No. I can't talk to you now. As I've said, I'm working.' I'm glad she's protecting our time together, but with an inward shiver: I would hate her to talk to me like that. I try to pick up the threads but she seems inattentive. Suddenly she bursts out, her cheeks flushing, 'I wish I had been more friendly. She was only collecting for something. And she sounded black. Oh dear.'

'Mustn't be unkind to our coloured brethren?'

She laughs. 'I'd like to invite her in for a cup of tea.'

I'm relieved to know that she's human and gets it wrong sometimes; and that the ice I heard in her voice can melt.

Another time she arrives looking flushed, her eyes sparking angrily. What have I done to cause this? I review my sins uneasily. After a few uncomfortable moments she says, 'I'm sorry, this is nothing to do with you. But I'm so angry.'

'What about?'

'I've just had a row with a GP. He doesn't think children's

feelings matter. Some of these GPs.' She smoulders. I breathe again. It's not me.

There is never any need to test or invoke reality. It insists on breaking through, disturbing our sacrosanct space. Usually it is my life: my leaving Nick, Mother's death, etc. But sometimes inevitably it is her life that obtrudes: visitors, neighbours met on the doorstep, workmen demanding attention. These she takes in her stride. But the death of her brother is sudden and unexpected; a brother to whom she was very close. I had met him on the stairs when he was visiting. She tells me about it quite openly. There is no hiding it. But she does not stop working.

A social worker friend opines that this is wrong. 'She can't possibly work in a properly professional way under such circumstances.'

'Who cares? I don't. I just want her to be there.'

What does professional mean? Who is it who can't cope, her or me? I can if she can. Honesty matters most. And to know whether my expectations of rejection are based in reality. I think I know her well enough by now to feel that she would take time off if she needed to. Of course she's not functioning in the same way. I'm not getting a hundred per cent of her attention. She's in a state of shock and it shows. But in a performance-related test I don't think I would score very high as a patient. I'm not complaining. She has to go through my stuff with me. Does it never work both ways? One of my problems with my own mother was that she presented an apparently infallible and unflappable surface. And my children have said the same about me in their early years.

She looks frozen: her cheeks pale, her eyes lack-lustre, looking into space, even her walk subdued. I don't know where she is but she isn't here. Mostly I keep quiet. But I do tell her what my friend has said. I'm not sure what she hears. She says coldly, 'I can't give you what you want at present. I can't give you as much as you want.'

I draw in a sharp breath and am surprised at how angry I feel. Forgetting consideration for her feelings I say crossly, 'Do you know what I want?'

A pause. 'No. I don't suppose I do.'

'Do you know how much I want?'

I have broken through her reserve. And get a slight smile. 'No.'

'I don't want anything from you. I just want to be allowed to stay here. I don't want you to send me away. And that's all I want.'

The atmosphere changes. She looks softer, a little more accessible, and says, 'Actually, you're a good person to be around when I feel like this.'

She says that a baby wants a perfect fit with its mother all the time. And is devastated when things go wrong. Learning to be separate is learning to tolerate the uncomfortable times, and to know that we can both survive.

But sometimes she's so crass! She says I'm ruthless.

I've had a row with an erstwhile 'best friend' and finished with her. I don't want her to be objective. I want her to be on my side. She should know that I'm right.

This friend has always been very demanding. And I've been there for her. But now it's my turn. I'm the one who is having a rough time. And my 'friend' can't cope, goes to pieces. I can't be bothered with her.

But she, Dr P, thinks I'm being hard. She says I'm very obstinate. 'Monolithically obstinate,' are her exact words.

Well so is she.

Whatever happened to the blank screen? Whatever happened to neutrality and empathy?

When I am not focused on seeing her I wander the city streets like a ghost drifting invisibly, directionless, taking no heed of where I am or where I'm going. I like to lose myself, and I like to think that no one knows where I am. As a companion this makes me quite amenable and I go wherever Jonah wants to go without argument. This evening, as often, we have walked a long way and are having a quiet drink in a pub before we go home. I ask idly what this pub is called. To my horror I realise that we are in the next street to Dr Penny's house. Rigid with panic I can look neither to the right nor to the left. Every time the door opens I expect her to walk in and say in tones of outrage and disdain, 'What are you doing here?' As soon as I am able I exit fast. I do tell her about that. She looks amused and asks why I think she would mind? 'Well it's your territory. I have no right to intrude.' 'But perhaps you'd like to.' What a suggestion!

vi

Time is slipping by. I feel old, I am old – well nearly, and tired. Wanting to do now what I should have been doing twenty years ago. Is it too late? Sometimes I think it isn't; I feel the sap rise in my veins just as it used to. Mostly I am sure it is.

Trying to make myself over I had to abandon the old life, and almost everyone connected with it. Hard enough to let myself be different. Impossible with people who liked me the way I was. I didn't believe they would let me change. I was more comfortable with strangers who had no precon-ceived ideas about me. I had to learn to live with myself. But it was lonely.

I met him on a long-distance train to Glasgow. Middle-aged, intelligent, charming; he sat opposite me and asked my opinion on some current issue that I've long forgotten.

He was a German businessman travelling for his firm in the UK. He was impressed with my honesty and my directness. He thought I was intelligent too; we could be great friends and have some wonderful conversations: he would teach me about Goethe, I would explain Shakespeare to him. He was married; he knew his wife would like me; I must come to dinner. A new friend. How exciting. We arranged to meet the following week when he was going to be in London. After a pleasant evening's wining and dining he drove me home.

It was truly delightful to find a woman with whom he had so much in common, he said.

'We are both experienced people' (speak for yourself, I thought) 'not romantic youngsters. Why don't we go to bed and add another dimension to our enjoyment of each other?' This wasn't what I intended.

'I don't think so,' I said, and added rather primly, 'I hardly know you. And what about your wife?'

'Oh, she wouldn't mind. We have a very free relationship; she has lovers too. It's not important. The most important thing is "the communion of true minds". But in the meantime why should we not enjoy our bodies too? Unless, of course, you are too inhibited or frigid?' Perish the thought. But he had overplayed his hand.

'No,' I said more firmly, 'I don't want to. Is that going to finish our friendship?'

'No, no, not at all. But it's a pity. I didn't think you would be so narrow-minded.' There was an awkward pause. 'In the meantime, please, just let me show you what I have to offer.' He took out his penis and began to masturbate. When I had regained my paralysed senses and my voice, I said, 'Please. Put it away,' and reaching for the car-door handle made my escape as rapidly as possible.

That marked the end of our wonderful friendship. He did phone once or twice more, but somehow we were never both free at the same time. I rushed back to Dr Penny the next day like any scared adolescent running to Mummy. My would-be sophistication didn't fool her for a moment. 'I think you are much more shocked than you are admitting.' She was right. It's not nice out there. What made me think I wanted to join in?

*

What happens to my words? Sometimes they die before they are uttered, futile, meaningless things. Sometimes they escape and die on an outward breath of exposure. Most often they fall to the ground, shot down like winged birds, dead on the carpet at her feet; like my eyes never to rise again. I am well acquainted with the colour and texture of her skirts: tweedy mixtures, heather colours I like.

I can talk. I have always been able to talk. Our family are good at that. I use words to camouflage, dissemble, parry, hide and justify. I envy those whose words march hand in hand with their feelings. I envy those with a gift for silence. I am in a cleft stick: I have neither the gift of silence nor the solace of words. Yes I can talk, but my words mean nothing if they are divorced from my feelings.

She uses words sparingly. When she does they have mean-ing, they convey something, they elucidate, illuminate, they strike home. She says my words convey more than I think. Sometimes she sees meanings in them that I don't. She remembers them, takes them seriously.

To me the space between us is an unbridgeable chasm; my words don't reach across. She says the space between us is the place where things happen. We both put things out there to be looked at, considered and examined, picked up, taken in, handed back, rejected even – but not ignored, not useless. My words do reach her. They don't just fall thud on the floor and die there. That brings me up against a paradox. Perhaps after all I prefer my words to be ignored. She is telling me that she takes them seriously, that they are important, that they have meaning. Now I am exposed, vulnerable, naked. My poor representatives are out there; they have escaped from prison; I can't take them back. Anything may happen: they may be reviled, scorned, derided, trodden underfoot, annihilated.

I contemplate this strange place, this space between us, this place where anything may happen. If there are rules she won't tell me. I may bark my shins finding out. Ah well, life is full of risk. She says it is the place where we play. Play? Play is for children. Well? Doesn't she know that 'Life is real! Life is earnest!'? I have rudely scorned all her suggestions for ways I might express my feelings. I am a teacher. I know all about the uses of clay, paint, sand and water. Of course, she says apologetically. But I can't actually do any of these things myself. I have never been what you might call creative. But as I contemplate this place, this space, this place where anything may happen, my fingers begin to itch. Can we have a playroom? A playroom? Yes, I would like a playroom. Suddenly I'm excited. When was I last excited? I could bring some plasticine, some coloured pens, some paper. She can produce paper and pen now, and does. This is very strange. This is fun. I can't draw but it doesn't matter. She joins in occasionally, reluctantly. When we have finished she puts all the things in a drawer till next time. I use plasticine the most; I like the way it feels, I don't have to think about it and it doesn't stop me talking.

When did we stop playing? I don't remember. Perhaps we didn't.

There was a place I went to when I felt rejected by and wanted to reject the whole world: a bleak sunless place, silent, uninhabited; a cold lonely unloving place, harsh and wild. But peaceful: no hurting, no misunderstanding, no duplicity. I was safe there. I was at home there. I could go there whenever I wanted. It was my retreat, the home of my despair. There it was understood and accepted.

There is a need to live a secret life that runs counter to the other, to the life of relating, of taking part, joining in, and being seen to do those things. Kept inside and denied, that secret life burst out and overwhelmed the other, spreading destruction, making the outer world match the inner desolation. Now I have turned inward, and ignoring the outer world live only inside myself. Their world is grey, encased in walls of glass. Their world makes demands of duty and obligation to keep the wheels turning; mine makes no demands, simply is; not hostile, not judging; indifferent, not caring if I live or die, leaving it up to me. My world is stripped to the bare essentials. My world is beautiful. My world does not hurt me. But I am afraid that I may not always be able to come back. One day I may die there alone.

Dr P accepted the reality of my experience, the truth of what I saw and heard and imagined, the images that came between me and the everyday world. She allowed them and therefore me to exist. Because she accepted them without argument I was able to trust her. And finally to tell her about the wasteland, as I called it. That was the last and most important of my secrets. And in the telling it became more real. Someone else knew about it, knew where I might be, knew where to look for me. I could go and come back. She could come to meet me, and perhaps if I got lost or stuck there she would come to look for me.

I dreamed of an attic where I lived, had lived for a long time. It was like my father's garden shed with rough walls of wooden planks and no window. It was full of clutter, indescribable unrecognisable junk covered with spiders' webs and the dust of ages. Like Miss Haversham without the wedding finery I sat in the ruins of what once had been a life. The air was fetid and stale. Through the slightly open door I could see the sky, clouds and patches of blue, feel the sunlight and a fresh breeze on my face. I was not ready to leave the safety of my attic yet. But one day I might. Or I might invite her in. She could help me sort through the clutter, get rid of some perhaps.

But then we had a misunderstanding.

I discovered the delight of saying no. No had always been impossible to say unless it was reinforced by a thousand good excuses. So the discovery that I could say no and the world didn't end – no one rushed screaming from the room – was truly liberating. Vistas of wilful caprice and self-indulgence. But not only that. When no was impossible, yes was often mere compliance, placatory, hypocritical. When no became possible then yes became a real choice, not just lip service. It was this I wanted to tell Dr P. It was like the opening of my attic door. I sensed a whole new world out there: a world of being myself, of knowing what I wanted and trying to get it. Up to now getting what I wanted had depended on someone else wanting it too. The people in the street seemed to reflect my changing mood; I looked at them with a new interest. Any one of them could be my friend. But I was still afraid of being ridiculed, though she never did. Mother would have said, 'If wishes were horses then beggars would ride.'

So I began hesitantly. I had realised, I said, that I didn't have to do anything I didn't want to. I could say no. If I wanted to I could go on saying no for ever. At which point an irritated Dr P said that I was mistaken if I thought she was going to sit there for the next twenty years while I said no. I felt as if I'd been punched in the stomach. I couldn't breathe, I couldn't speak. For the rest of the session I sat with my knees drawn up and my hands over my face. There was nothing but pain.

After a long time she began to talk. I couldn't hear what she said but I heard her voice which was kind and gentle, not irritated, not scornful, not angry. Slowly the pain lessened and I could speak. I took my hands away from my face but I couldn't look at her.

'Do you mind that you hurt me?'

'Yes. Very much.'

It was as if I'd brought her a basket of good things and she had thrown them on the floor without bothering to look

at them. I'd brought some writing and a poem to show her
as well. I did tell her the poem before I left. If I'd started
with it we might have avoided the misunderstanding:

> When I wake in the morning
> and know how alone I am
> I know how long I have been alone.
> So long my bones are fossils,
> unused to the accommodating curve
> of another body: petrified, brittle,
> having lain through rigid nights
> a guardian to pain.
> Handle me gently.
> The curator of the museum
> must unwrap with care
> the layers of cold uncaring years
> that have preserved untouched
> a memory of living flesh,
> of a girl that ran and danced,
> who felt the caress of sun and wind,
> and knew the touch of a human hand
> for a moment. And forgot.
> Otherwise my bones may snap
> and crack with pain
> and the marrow fall away
> to dust in your hand.

Dr P's irritation was understandable. I had been saying no
to her for a long time tacitly. She said she thought I was
stuck, when we talked about it later. She'd wanted to bring
the deathbed nearer. But it was some time before I was able
to open the door to my attic again. And the people in the
street were strangers once more.

But something had happened that had to happen if we
were to move on: the direct experience of a misunderstanding between us and, however painful, being able to sort it
out and effect a reconciliation. Previously I would have gone

away and dealt with the hurt and the anger by myself until I had it under control.

So I learned painfully. Controlling my feelings, never knowing the relief of expressing them and the comfort of another's sympathy, had intensified the pain, not lessened it as it was intended to, and as I always expected it would. Far from being impervious to hurt I used to feel that I had been born with a layer of skin too few.

*

Jessica, Lottie and I are coming back from the theatre one Saturday night.

As we emerge from the station the rain is just beginning, large drops splattering heavily on the forecourt, a slight steam rising from the paving stones. A freak summer storm is coming. The air is heavy and stifling. In our thin cotton dresses we shall get wet. We decide to make a dash for it. The flat is only a few minutes away.

When we are halfway along the High Street the clouds open. A jagged corkscrew of lightning hits the pavement ahead and almost simultaneously we are engulfed in a deluge, as if someone is emptying a bucket over us, rain pouring down in sheets. With a scream I rush for the nearest shop doorway, followed by my dripping exhilarated daughters. Overhead the thunder rolls and booms. I cower in the corner hiding my head, covering my ears.

Surprised Jessica says, 'Are you frightened?'

'Terrified,' I mutter between stiff lips.

Lottie puts her arms around me. 'Why you're shaking. It's allright, you're quite safe.'

Jessica puts her arms round too. It feels so good to be hugged and comforted. By my children? I should be ashamed. But it's such a relief to let go and simply be frightened. (All those years of pretending!)

The storm passes as suddenly as it came, leaving the pavements steaming and the air rapidly cooling. As we hurry home I am strangely lighthearted. Fear has been survived. And has vanished as if it had never been.

From the bottom of the pit I look out at a ravaged landscape. There are ruined houses. Ivy has grown over some of them, softening the harsh outlines. Trees have sprung up around them. I wander through large mansions, through numberless dark empty rooms. Looking for what? I don't know. In this dreamworld, in which it is always night and moonlight is the only light, there are never any people.

As I sit on the ground a piece of wood falls at my feet, apparently from the sky. It is a varnished plaque, the kind they sell in souvenir shops. Inscribed on it in burnt poker work are the words: 'In my Father's house are many mansions.' What kind of a message is that? And from a God I don't believe in. I've seen enough empty rooms. Maybe it's a joke. I always thought he must have a peculiar sense of humour. I smile sardonically.

(I am writing doggerel verse around this time, about the Sleeping Beauty and Rapunzel, hidden away in solitary seclusion by the wicked witch, waiting for the prince to come and rescue them. Only in my version he never comes. I've stopped believing in happy endings.)

I attend an art workshop where we draw with crayons on large sheets of paper, like children. Artistic achievement is unimportant; the point is to explore images and symbols of our emotions and our dreams. From time to time we are asked to draw ourselves as we are at this moment. I always draw myself sitting on the ground inside a cave. Outside it is sunny with flowers and trees and a river. But I prefer to stay inside looking out on it all from my safe dark cave.

I suppose it counts as progress when I draw myself inside a telephone booth. I am more visible. And the means of communication are at hand even if I don't appear to be using them.

Then the fires came raging through the buildings, gutting them, razing them to the ground. It is satisfying to see the flames consuming everything in their path and afterwards to contemplate the flattened landscape. Mine is the power, mine the anger that rages and consumes and burns and demolishes.

One afternoon I was lying on my bed dozing when a rag and bone man drove his horse and cart down the street. Instead of, 'Any old rags', I thought he was calling, 'Bring out your dead.' I fell asleep and dreamed that I was packing all my dead bodies into a coffin. Then I carted them off to the crematorium. I watched them burning glad to be rid of them. But as the flesh fell away from the bones a tiny foetus was revealed. I was haunted by the idea that it might have been alive. But it was too late, I had already destroyed it.

I had stopped pretending. I felt more real. The world I had failed in receded. I was living more and more in my own world inside my own reality, mourning my failure and accepting the enormity of it, not trying to deny it any more. A lifetime of living in the light of reason was reversed and I had tumbled headlong into the abyss. Was this the price I had to pay? What was the foetus I had inadvertently destroyed? Perhaps it was too late. It was preferable but it could also be dangerous. Would I ever come out of it or would I be stuck for ever in the shadowlands of past grief and present fantasy?

*

I have been in analysis a long time. How long it's difficult to remember. It must be nine years.

Some things have changed: I am more in charge of my life, I can cope with people better. I understand that I have never separated from my mother, never become independent, and that I repeat the way I was with her with everyone.

But inside I feel no different. Change is not happening to me as I hoped it would. Inside I am as unhappy and self-doubting and nihilistic as I ever was. The only difference is that I am more open about it, more vocal. It's no use pretending, I'm never going to change.

Friends tell me it's taking far too long, I've become too dependent on her. That's what they do to you these psychiatrists. You have to get on and live your own life. Whoopee! If only I could.

Yes I am dependent on her. She knows how it is and just how much help I need to get by. She believes in me when I don't believe in myself. She has hope for me when I have none. She doesn't tell me to pull myself together and get on with it. She knows how little joy I have in life and how much in love with death I am. My biggest fear is that she will lose patience with me and tell me to go. She is still my only hope.

Today I move to the other side of the room, as far away from her as I can get. I have to tell her that we have failed. I can't put it off any longer.

I say, 'On the one hand I understand everything you say and I believe it. I know it's true. But on the other I have to say that I don't believe a word of it. It's not true for me. If it is true it makes no difference to me.'

I've just demolished all our work. I'm standing near the door so I can make a run for it.

There's a pause, and then she says quietly, matter of factly, 'Well let's talk about that then.'

I walk slowly back to my chair. She isn't even offended.

I had graduated, if that's the right word, to sitting on the couch. Lying down, the correct analytic posture terrified me. A chair gave me support, protection and a semblance of autonomy. Sitting on the couch was a compromise and a sort of progress. It also brought me nearer to her. I had mixed feelings about that.

But there was still this gap, a chasm it felt like between us: unbridgeable in spite of any understanding or insight: facile words. The more I longed to be close to her the more I was stuck, incapable of spontaneous movement, any movement. She sat looking warmly attentive and relaxed — and out of reach. I had told her how I felt.

Suddenly she held out a hand: 'Could this be a bridge?'

I shrank back and stared at her hand in horror. The silence lengthened and she dropped her hand. I was mortified and ashamed. I had rejected her. She wouldn't try again.

It sounds odd to say that we practised holding hands. But that's what we did.

It wasn't like riding a bike. It didn't come back to me in a flash. I couldn't remember that I had ever wanted to or why I should.

I remember holding Mother's hand when we went shopping and crossing the road. I was sorry when I got too big to do that. Holding hands with boy friends didn't seem to count — it was usually initiated by them. I don't remember when Nick and I last held hands. Touching usually led on to sex, and that had made me wary. But then he went off sex and we didn't touch at all, unless I had a nightmare and reached out for him as I woke. Then he would hold me until I calmed down. Holding hands, holding anything seemed to be something that was done to me rather than by me

The first time I managed to put my hand out and grasp hers it was like an electric shock. The whole of my arm was galvanised by pins and needles. My hand was frozen, numb and lifeless. By contrast hers was warm and dry, not grasping or clinging, but strong and comforting, if I could let it be.

Hearing the Beatles on the radio singing about holding hands, I burst into tears.

It did get easier.

Slowly my landscape altered.

When we began, Dr Penny and I, the skies were always grey; on the hottest day I was cold; a cloud obscured the sun and dulled its brightness: a veil of depression between me and what they said was the real world.

After the fires had died out the rains came; like the first deluge drowning and washing away houses, trees, everything, obliterating and flattening the landscape to a monochrome expanse of undefined land and sea. An occasional treetop raising its head above the water a forlorn reminder of living form.

I drown in tears. Are they God's or mine? I cry for what I have made. I cry for the sad and the lonely. God should cry for what he has made. There is no end to crying.

The rains receding left a sea of mud. Familiar landmarks have disappeared. It looks like the primeval swamp from which the first life emerged.

To feel the mud between my toes and squeeze it through my fingers is to be a child again squatting close to the earth making mud pies. It brings back those holidays on Canvey Island: the wide expanses of mud before we reached the sea. Brings back the smell and the satisfying feel of it. Brings back a time when the world was a safe place and God was a man with a long grey beard who looked like Daddy.

One day the sun shines, the sky is blue, the wind lifts my hair and green shoots break through the mud. Life is beginning again. In the wake of death and devastation life renews itself. It is like a miracle. I don't have to do a thing. Life happens. And will always happen with or without my participation. I have been like those South American Indians who thought they had to get up in the morning to help the sun rise. I don't have to try so hard. Life will happen to me too if I let it. I am just one small part of it: no more, no less.

Part III

For once, then, something

Robert Frost

i

The world of imagination, of fairytale and myth, the world of the poets came to my rescue. Poets understand about the razor-sharp line between sanity and insanity, between hope and despair, between reality and unreality. I let my feelings spill out on paper. Extreme feelings may be harnessed and expressed in a form that makes them more acceptable and gives them some purpose other than mere disembarrassment. Removed from my orbit they entered another domain. They acquired a life of their own, a more objective existence. Sometimes I could even let them go. But that brought another danger. What would happen when they were removed from my protection? What harm that I might be powerless to prevent? Attacked and destroyed, or worse ignored and discarded. They were my defenceless children.

Coming home on the bus from Lottie's one night with an empty suitcase that she had borrowed, I left it in the cubby hole at the bottom of the stairs while I went upstairs to smoke. It was a cheap, battered case of no value and contained nothing but a few pages of my writing. I felt increasingly uneasy, watching the people who got off at each stop in case anyone pinched it. I was forced finally to go downstairs and sit, cigaretteless, where I could keep my eye on it. I felt ridiculous and was glad there were no witnesses to my absurdity. It wasn't the case but my writing that I was worried about. Why should it matter if anyone stole what I generally regarded as rubbish?

One story that I wrote held particular meaning for me; I had no idea why. A princess had been hidden in a castle on a remote island by the king, her father, to keep her safe from his enemies. The castle was surrounded by a deep moat and guarded by lions. She was alone there with the king's trusted servants. One day he would come and reclaim her. It was lonely waiting but she was buoyed up by the thought of his return. Much time went by. The retainers grew old and died. The lions lost their teeth and grew thin and hungry. The princess was growing old. Her father would not come now. He must have died. She waited for death to come to her too. But was surprised by the arrival of a witch. The witch befriended her, took her off the island on her broomstick and showed her how to get by in the outside world. The witch was kind but untidy and rather fat. And not infallible: her spells did not always work. But she meant well, and said that she would accompany the princess on her journey wherever it led. The princess knew that one day she would have to go back to the island, face the lions and rescue them. And when she did she knew that the witch would go with her. As a talisman the witch gave her a beautiful ring.

I knew that the witch was Dr P., though my description of her owed more to malice than to accuracy. It was very important to me to know that she would go with me wherever I went. I had liked Jung ever since I heard him say that the doctor must be prepared to go with the patient wherever the patient might need to go.

In other stories the witch was purely malevolent, seeking to destroy the heroine who was always a little girl. Escape was only by a hair's breadth and danger was ever present.

In dreams the evil witch was my mother waiting in the dark to jump out at me, clinging on to my back, trying to strangle me. Even after her death she still haunted me. I would dream that she was not really dead but just hiding, under the bed or behind the door.

Now she was the bad one and Dr P was all good. I had discovered my lost anger. It was all directed at her. I hated her. In my dreams I wrestled with her; in the sessions I railed against her. But in reality she was an old woman, frail and ill. I was never able to show her any but my customary pleasant face.

My father was remote. Like the king in my story he was never able to rescue me. He was kind and generous, funny and clever and selfish. As the breadwinner he was not to be disturbed or bothered: a true Victorian. I think the mystique that surrounded him was put there by Mother mostly, he just took advantage of it. He was not a conceited man. But he was rarely at home. Like Mother he was a dedicated worker for a socialist future: secretary of the local Labour Party and always out at meetings. He was also very involved in the administration of the Woodcraft Folk. Only when he was old and ill after Mother had died were we able to be close. But even that was dictated by his needs, not mine.

ii

I had always been drawn to those children who experienced difficulties at school, behavioural or academic. When I was still a young and inexperienced teacher, and remedial teaching was hardly recognised as such, I had been put in charge of a class of thirty children, aged from six to thirteen years, because I was perceived as being 'good' with them. The head's only proviso was that I must keep them quiet and not offend their parents. Their problems were as various as inherent retardation and the traumatic effects of the war: one six-year-old had been buried under rubble for hours − he had a severe stutter; another lived on chips and bread and jam − all his mother, depressed by her husband's absence, could manage.

Michael, a diminutive eight-year-old, halted in mid-flight by my voice, stands between me and the classroom door. I feel exasperated and helpless that someone so small can prove so impossible to control.

This is a repeated occurrence. Michael had been evacuated

and returned practically a stranger to a mother who has her hands full with a new baby and no time for him. To every attempt to correct either his sums or his behaviour he has one response: 'Fuck off.' He spends all his time drawing violent pictures of war: bombs exploding, aeroplanes bursting into flames. Almost the only word he can read is 'aeroplane'.

When things get too much for him he bolts. Aware of my responsibility for him and that I cannot leave my class to follow him, in desperation I say, 'If you step outside the classroom door I will cane you.' What a stupid thing to say! How can I? To my surprise he returns to his desk and gives me no more trouble that day.

I battled and wept after school and finally won through in a hit-and-miss sort of way. We learnedtogether and in the end were a happy class, and those who could even learned a little. Some of my methods would not be approved of now. For instance, swearing was very much objected to by some parents: I washed a couple of mouths out with soap and water (Michael was the first), and the swearing stopped. They bore me no grudge. Nor I them for all the kicks and blows I fielded. When a battle was over that was it. I sometimes wonder how we survived. I remember them with great affection.

Paul was the teacher in charge of the Remedial Unit. I had been able to increase the hours I worked there and resume payment of Dr P's proper fees.

It was a good place to work. I had a small room of my own and didn't have to mix with the other members of staff unless I wished to. The building was an old condemned infants' school, divided up and added on to. It held unhappy memories of myself as a young teacher, bullied by an authoritarian headmistress prone to violent outbursts of rage. The building was now owned by the Health Authority and part of it leased to the Education Department.

Fortunately I was in the new wing. We were a mixed bag:

psychiatrist, psychologist, social workers and teachers. The mixture worked very well. We were all concerned with remedying damaged lives in one way or another, very often working with the same families. I did not feel out of place.

Paul knew that I was in analysis and kept a sympathetic and dispassionate eye on me. I was aware, particularly when I was working with a difficult child, that he found more reason to knock on my door than was strictly necessary.

There was a day when I couldn't go on. I rang Paul and told him. I had flu, but I didn't somehow take that into account. He asked if he could contact Dr P.

Everyone was kind. Jonah who hated interruptions at work said I could phone him whenever I needed to. Lottie came to look after me. Paul said he would expect to see me in two weeks' time. I just wanted to be left alone. I couldn't stand everyone being so kind. When the flu was better I picked myself up and went back to work.

Dr P said she'd told Paul to put as much pressure on me as the work demanded. We would pick up the pieces. Unfeeling monster. I wanted her to look after me and tell them all to go away. But she was always in favour of me working (worried about her fees?).

Paul seemed to know when it was the right moment to nudge me out of my isolation, suggesting that I join them for lunch in the staffroom. Gradually I thawed out in the non-judgemental atmosphere I found there.

I was still working with Jane, the last of my home-tuition pupils, who had severe epilepsy. Dr Craig, the Medical Officer of Health, came to discuss Jane's future.

I had known Dr Craig for a long time. She was the doctor in charge of the baby clinic when Jessica and Lottie were born. I remembered her as comforting and reassuring to anxious young mothers. She knew all my family, including Nick, through their work on the local council. We had not met for some years. She was shocked at my appearance. I had lost a lot of weight. She said I looked ill and should have an X-ray on my chest. It was not the time or the place for explanations. Jane's mother who knew nothing of my situation said, 'Well you have fallen away.'

A strange idiom, but it seemed apt and stayed in my mind.

> I have fallen away from the girl that I was,
> from the soft eager youth that was mine.
> I have crushed the glittering bauble I held
> and the pieces still cling to my hand.
> Fragile and brittle I see them fall
> as the withering years
> that have fallen away from my soul.

Dr Craig invited me to her home to discuss Jane further. I told her that I had left Nick. She commented only that she had always thought he and my mother were very alike. They both had rigid, inflexible personalities. A new idea. One that neither of them would have liked.

*

Sometimes the only way to ensure that you get to a place on time, particularly a place you don't want to go but know you have to, is to start out very early. Then you can avoid all the obstacles that life or you yourself may throw in your way. That was how I discovered the coffee-drinking coterie.

I have a job for one year in a primary school that has the highest illiteracy in the borough. I take groups of children from every class for reading lessons. I am popular with the children and with the teachers for removing for a while the burden of striving and strife.

As usual I like most of the children. I like some of the teachers. I hate being there. I hate schools: smelly, gloomy places with rules I am supposed to enforce: don't talk, don't run, don't make a mess, don't – whatever you are about to do. I am too depressed to care. It takes me all my time to stay there myself.

I walk through the twilight and the rain of an early winter morning. It always seems to be raining. The only other weather I remember is snow: the most severely depressed and withdrawn boy in the school rushing up to me with shining eyes to show me a miracle – on his gloved hand a single snowflake. 'Look Miss, look at the pattern.'

I hide beneath my umbrella my reluctance and my morning face. The few children that are about don't notice me. The other remedial teacher rushes in at the last minute: cheerful, enthusiastic and dedicated.

Arriving early because otherwise I may not arrive at all, I find the staffroom almost empty. It is an unlovely room. The furnishings are as dog-eared as the textbooks. One member of staff stands with her back to the room, busy with a kettle and the coffee mugs. She raises a finger in greeting. Gradually others drift in. The early ones are mostly the single, the widowed and the divorced or those who are simply eager to get away from home. No one says more than is absolutely necessary, and no one feels obliged to smile. This is a great find. I almost look forward to the mornings. If only they weren't followed by the rest of the day.

*

> *We make ourselves a place apart*
> *Behind light words that tease and flout.*
> *But oh, the agitated heart*
> *Till someone really find us out.*
>
> Robert Frost

Bringing the two worlds, internal and external, into coexistence seemed impossible and highly dangerous; I might be destroyed in the process.

Dr P and I had begun to build a bridge across which I inched reluctantly and fearfully towards her. Like those rope and bamboo constructions that sway perilously across a deep ravine in the jungle it was the only means of communication between the two sides. One slash of a knife, in our case one misplaced word, and the whole precarious structure plunges to the rocks below and the traveller is lost for ever.

Apart from Dr P, and my children who were there by right, and Jonah who ignored them, Myrtle was the first to penetrate my defences. It was typical of her that she trod where others feared or more probably didn't care to go.

Off work with bronchitis, a biennial occurrence. It was a bleak February day, snow turning to sleet, cold and damp. I returned home with my prescription from the chemist to find her standing on my doorstep holding a large bunch of chrysanthemums.

'I was worried about you. I thought I'd pop round and see if there was anything I could do. Or maybe just cheer you up.' Faced with my dismayed silence Myrtle's smile faded. 'Of course if it's not convenient, I'll just leave the flowers and go. I expect you don't feel like visitors.' She sounded hurt.

'No I don't really,' I blurted out, and then appalled at my rudeness said sorry and practically dragged her upstairs. I sat her down with her back to my unmade bed and explained that I was ashamed of the mess, and that I'd become very anti-social and she was my first visitor, and it was nothing personal but I didn't want her to see the way I lived.

Looking immaculate in the midst of my squalor, which she said she didn't mind at all, and smoking a rare cigarette, she talked about her breakdown after her husband's death when she couldn't bear to see people.

That was the beginning of our friendship.

A gentle but firm tap on the door. It's the lunch hour. Why can't they leave me alone?

A steaming cup appears around the door followed by Myrtle's smiling face.

'I've brought you a cup of tea, dear. I thought perhaps you wouldn't feel up to joining us today. So I thought I'd bring it along and see how you are.'

I am dying for a cuppa, but she's quite right. Wild horses wouldn't drag me into the staffroom today.

'Well, no I wasn't going to bother.'

She perches herself neatly on the edge of my desk. Everything Myrtle does is neat and composed, even when her arthritis is paining her.

'Not so good today?'

'No,' I mumble feeling furtive. 'I'm a bit low.'

'Saw you coming down the road this morning. Said to myself, there's a depressed walk if ever I saw one. You were going so slowly it's a wonder you managed to arrive at all.'

'I did have a job to get myself here.'

Myrtle clucked sympathetically. 'I know how you feel. I'll leave you to it then. Give me a knock at home time. We could have a drink if you like.'

And she did know. That was the lovely and surprising thing about Myrtle inside her sometimes severe and straight-laced appearance. She never pried or sought to moralise. She knew that my marriage had broken up, that was all. What she understood without need of explanation was how it feels when life has no point and just keeping going from one day to the next requires a superhuman effort.

Myrtle had married late in life. Her husband had died suddenly and unexpectedly after several very happy years together. She had been devastated. I first met her at the Remedial Unit when, looking grim but not complaining, she was beginning to pick up the pieces of her life again. It was clear that her *raison d'être* had died with her husband. I get no false cheer from Myrtle, only unobtrusive kindness and a willing ear.

Dorothy provides me with a bolt hole. She is one of my

oldest friends, the only one I am still in touch with. When things get beyond me and I can no longer stand my own company I take a train into rural Sussex to her large untidy house. Dorothy is a widow with two small children. Not waiting even to phone her I sometimes end up sitting on her doorstep in the dark until she comes home. She asks no questions; plies me with food and drink and distracting chatter and gossip.

We share a taste for the ridiculous. She leads a fascinating and hair-raising love life with someone else's husband. Can she bring him to stay in my flat for the weekend — while I am somewhere else naturally? Since her husband's sudden death from a heart attack Dorothy has a morbid fear of the same thing happening again. We collapse in giggles at the thought of her lover stretched out naked and dead on the floor of my bedsitting room. I hardly know how. How would I explain his presence?

Dr P could exist in both worlds, theirs and mine, moving easily between them unafraid, though she understood my anxiety. To me their world was grey and insubstantial; vague figures mouthing silently behind a wall of glass. Mine was black, shot through with streaks of colour — rather like a Jackson Pollock painting. I preferred mine; however unpleasant, it was at least real. You know you exist when it hurts.

When she went away I was lost, floundering like a beached whale. I rang her the evening before her holiday.

'How is it that you have hope and I have not? When you go, you take it all away.'

'It's your hope. I keep it for you. Like a bank. For you to draw on when you're ready.'

Imperceptibly and very slowly the fragmented pieces began to move towards each other and join together again.

Hope had been mooted, its presence suggested; like the

change in the darkness that precedes the dawn, the restlessness of birds when a tentative call breaks the silence; a prelude
to the day.

I lived in darkness and total despair but its opposite was
out there somewhere beyond the horizon, though as yet out
of sight.

iii

This was the view, so to speak, from within Dr P. In the safe
circle of her arms I could contemplate disaster and death and
the perils of renewal without being engulfed and lost for
ever. Like it or not she was my mother. She gave birth to
my real self. She might perhaps say that she assisted me in
finding what was already there but had got lost or stopped
working properly. But these are just words. She was more
than a midwife, more than a doctor presiding over a delivery.
She held me safe within her, with all my grief, with all my
pain, my weakness, my inability, my ugliness, my hate,
my rage, my spleen, my spite. She held me until I healed:
until gaping wounds closed, until new skin could grow. She
put a 'green and healing finger in my wound'.

Mother's help rendered me helpless, her power made me
powerless. I had to learn that it isn't either or, but both.
Growing up is not taking over the role of the omnipotent
parent, not the role reversal that was all I knew, but struggling
to meet other equally fallible people on equal terms.

I had never truly been a child. I had been a pseudo-adult,
mother's standard-bearer, an extension of her. The child in
me existed in timidity and shyness, in irresponsibility and
laziness of which I was ashamed. But the confident child, the
fearless, exploring, curious, life-loving child, that child had

died. It lived on for me in other people, most of all in my children. But never in myself until now.

She was a good mother: hardworking, conscientious, strict but kindly, and where other people's mistakes were concerned generous and compassionate; for her own she had no mercy. Living in her shadow the same high standards were demanded of me. Failure could not be tolerated. There was only one way to do everything, the right way, and that meant her way. It had nothing to do with individual desire or personality and temperament. She could brook no disagreement. If we did differ, which was rare, the failure to understand had to be mine. To be comfortable again I had only to admit that I was wrong and harmony was restored. 'If you can't beat 'em, join 'em.'

So compassion for myself and my mistakes had to begin with Dr P. She validated my experience, my way of being: not right or wrong, just mine. She said, 'It's important for you to make your own decisions. If I tell you what to do I'm being like your mother.' Of course I wanted her to tell me, but at the same time I didn't. I had to reject what she said. Having believed that Mother knew best, and finding that that wasn't so, I wasn't about to be taken in again. I could take nothing for granted. Which made it difficult for Dr P.

I had been taught that life is about accepting what you are given, making the best of it, learning to like it: lying on the bed you have made. I had yet to learn that ultimately life is about survival, and that is not necessarily nice. It isn't about waiting to be asked and accepting what you're given; more often about grabbing and taking (without waiting, or someone else may get there first), pushing and shoving, fighting and kicking – all the things that had been most frowned on – or at least acknowledging the impulse.

Reality; wholeness – catchwords. But most important catchwords. Nothing to do with being good, or even with being happy. Everything to do with being able to distinguish between illusion and reality. Truth is subjective and many-faceted. I can only see through my own short-sighted eyes, speak with my own limited voice. Reality may be painful but it is always preferable to illusion, though I don't always know one from the other. Wholeness is something I go towards but never achieve, as it has to include as many different aspects of myself as I can tolerate – especially the bits I don't like. It is within myself that the lion has to lie down with the lamb. It is I who have to differentiate real guilt and real responsibility from their illusory counterparts. As the old song says: 'I am myself my own fever and pain.'

My strength is my weakness,
my weakness my strength,
my pleasure too often my pain –
the lion in the lamb and vice-versa.
That is the paradox.
Living it is individuation, becoming sane.
But the lamb that goes roaring to the shepherd,
the lion that goes bleating to the kill
is likely to be misunderstood.

*

I have been skirting around perhaps the most important issue of all. But it has to be faced, as it was eventually with Dr P. Can or indeed should an analyst/psychotherapist love his or her patient? I'm not talking about love in the way that people do who think they 'love' everybody. That is so generalised as to be meaningless. I'm talking about an intensity of feeling towards a particular person that can be a source of great happiness or misery.

The need for love is a hunger, greater or less according to the degree of its previous absence. How do you measure it? How do you even know what you are missing if it is outside your experience, and all you know is there is something inside you that remains unsatisfied? How do you learn what it is? And where do you go to find out if not to the one person who has managed to help you so far when everything and everyone else has failed?

Love had become a dirty word to me. My parents loved me as parents do, or as parents should. They told me so and I believed them. But I didn't feel loved, I didn't feel lovable, and now I didn't feel loving.

When I was young I experienced their love as protection, but also as an expectation and a demand that I never managed to live up to. As I grew older it became a burden, a duty, a debt that I could never finish paying. It stopped me living my own life. As long as they needed me I had to be there.

They said, 'We don't want to be a burden.' Which translated for me meant, 'Don't tell us we are a burden.'

Why did I stay? Could I do without them? Who needed whom the most? Did I think if I stayed long enough they might give me what I wanted?

As I experienced it, love was conditional, not freely given. I didn't want that any more. I wanted something very badly but I didn't know what. I could only define it by what I didn't want. It mustn't be possessive, it mustn't demand unquestioning loyalty, it mustn't try to define me or tell me how I should be. It must let me be: that was the first thing. It must not lie: honesty was more important than kindness. I wanted to be told the truth and to be able to tell it myself. Love with all its invisible ties had let me down. So love went out of the window. It was not enough.

However an eminent psychologist talking on the radio made me know how I really felt. Patients, he said, want from their analyst the kind of love only a mother can give, but this is neither possible nor desirable. A patient must not ask his analyst to love him. I heard myself saying, 'but she has to'. Whatever the rules said that was what I wanted. I couldn't wait to ask her if she agreed with him. She was noncommittal, but said he wasn't necessarily right. I carefully avoided asking her if she did love me; I expected her to say no. But it was most important to be allowed to want her to, to keep the subject open. I would have been devastated if she had agreed with him.

I did want her to love me. But it had to be as I wanted. I knew my parents loved me. That wasn't the problem. But they didn't know and weren't able to give me what I needed.

So what did I want?

Hidden deep inside me was a small cowering shameful creature, ugly and unlovable, that had never seen the light of day, had never been able to lift its head and look around and say here I am. That she had to love; to hold, to nourish, to let be, to let grow. No small task. I fought her every inch of the way. I couldn't have put it into words, but I had a conviction of the enormity of what I wanted and the impossibility of getting it. The feeling that I asked too much. In fact I asked very little, Dr P said. But in a way it was true. I demanded endless time, endless patience. I didn't know what it was I lacked but I knew when I hadn't got it. I'd never had enough, whatever that meant. Moderation in all things seemed to mean satisfaction in none. I wanted to have too much, so much that I could be careless with it; be fractious and capricious, discard some, reject some and still come back for more. I didn't always want to start with brown bread and butter. Sometimes I wanted to start with cake, go on with cake and finish with cake.

There was a world from which I was excluded. I didn't belong. I had always known that. Other people did, or behaved as if they did, as if they and the things they did were important. I pretended. I went along. I 'passed' for one of them. And as long as they were around it was all right. But when they went away I ceased to exist. Life was simply a space to fill, time to pass, a day to get through. It was like an eternal interview for a job you've never going to get. It's not worth living if all it ever is, is an ordeal to be got through.

With Dr P time developed a new significance. It was this

moment now that mattered: what was happening in it, what I wanted from it, how I felt about it. Now, not yesterday, not tomorrow. Not wishing my life away but examining it, exploring it, as if this might be the only moment we have. Like a child for whom time has no meaning because all time is now.

She provided a space, a safe place where I could simply be, where we could be together and find the limits and the boundaries of ourselves and each other, discover its finite shape and its infinite possibilities, bump against each other, meet and collide, and most importantly simply be.

Habits of thought, attitudes, behaviour over the years become engrained, woven into the fabric, even fossilised. Not like a shell that can be broken, from which the true, the radiant self may burst forth undamaged (to the sound of loud applause). Such was my secret fantasy. Rationally I didn't think I could change at all. The reality was somewhere in between.

iv

I had been seeing Dr Penny for nine years. Life had changed considerably. But I was still isolated and lonely, and still taking anti-depressants, though a much reduced dosage.

In February I went north to stay with Jessica for the mid-term break. She was living in the basement of a once grand old house with high-ceilinged rooms and draughts. Most of the tenants, like the house, had seen better days. Jessica liked the privacy. No one bothered anyone else. And it was cheap.

She has gone to work. Many feet have hurried past the

railings of the basement area, have gone clack-clacking over the worn flagstones, and now the street is empty.

I'm sitting huddled in the depths of a badly sprung arm-chair smoking a cigarette, looking out, my mind as empty as the street and the unbroken stretch of time ahead. I have nothing to do until Jessica comes home. There is nothing I want to do. I may sit here all day. How many aeons have I spent sitting thus, slumped like a rag doll that someone has thrown down and forgotten?

Across the street a dog lifts its leg at the base of a tree. A shower of raindrops falls silently to the ground shining in the weak sun that has managed to straggle through the clouds. I can almost smell the damp freshness of the air even in this stale atmosphere. It is the time of year when winter still hesitates to give way to spring. The clouds are shifting now and a pearl-grey wash spreads across the sky.

A surge of energy goes through me and suddenly I want to be out there. I throw on some warm clothes and make my way to the park. Muted greens and browns, sodden leaves under bare black branches on patient trees. The river flows sullenly swollen with rain under the grey stone bridge. Flakes of white on the grass are snowdrops breaking through. Clean after the rain a veil of dirt and grime has been pulled aside and I breathe in the new life that is stirring under the surface as it is stirring in me.

God or whatever is offering me this gift, this day newly created. And I am open to it, taking it in, savouring it, even the cold air a caress on my cheek. I am here. And I am happy. The long winter of mourning is over.

I carry this feeling inside me carefully like a delicate-shelled egg that may easily break.

I didn't expect it to last. Such moments had happened before. I waited apprehensively for the drab veil to descend again. But everything stayed as it was. And with the world newborn came an access of energy that carried me all over that grubby northern town and out into the surrounding countryside. Jessica was astonished at the change in me, at my enthusiasm and my interest in things. For so long I had been narrowly and grimly focused inwards.

This was not a momentary escape from misery. This was new, the feeling of being a part of everything, not just the beautiful; equally the squalid and ugly. In the High Road stood the solid municipal offices and elegant Edwardian houses built for prosperous merchants. Under railway arches in the more seedy part of town, second-hand clothes were spread out on plastic sheets. Tired women and dirty-faced children raked through the piles of worn clothing, exchanging the worn for the only slightly less worn. Following the river in its course a well-landscaped walkway passed through the back streets and playing fields to end abruptly where the fields and hedges of the rural landscape took over. From there I could see the hills inky blue in the distance as the afternoon darkened.

I was somewhere in all of this, from the solidity of my sturdy ancestors – solicitors, builders and farmers – to my identification with the lowest of the low – the helpless, the hopeless, those who would never amount to much. In it, of it, with it, but apart from it. For the first time not overwhelmed by obligation, by ties of duty or affection, responsibility or guilt: dispassionate, disinterested: my own person. The world had at last become centred in me and I in it. I looked out upon it and knew myself to be and wanting to be a part of it. And knew it was there for me to partake of.

Part IV

'For no one thinks unless a complex makes him'

W. H. Auden

'Good fences make good neighbours'

Robert Frost

i

I returned from that holiday full of energy and resolve. Life was about to begin. It had of course been going on all the while, but now I wanted to join in. I felt myself turning towards people instead of away from them; hungry for them; and impatient to get on with it. I was like a child to whom every experience is new and exciting.

Travelling to London the railway lines glimmered dully in the subdued afternoon light. As we approached the station they multiplied, crossing and recrossing, weaving elaborate patterns, appearing and reappearing, shunting us effortlessly from one to another. Yesterday they had been only carrying me to a place I didn't want to go. Today they are a metaphor for the whole journey, humming, pulsating with life. I had felt that beat when I was young, and the sense of impending adventure that I feel now is the same as then. The other travellers look tired and bored, their faces shuttered. I pity them. They have the look of people who have lost what I had lost but now have found again.

My father: eighty five years old, indomitable and adaptable, had survived Mother's death by six years. At first he was very clinging. He had never been without a woman to look after him, and for fifty years that woman had been Mother. He took it for granted that I would fill her place. But finally accepted, if he didn't understand, my need to live alone. He had never been ill, never been depressed. Telling him that I wouldn't live with him was one of the most difficult things I ever had to do. Living with him, my financial worries would have been at an end. But I would have been back in the same dependent position that I had been in all my life.

He was hurt. It hadn't occurred to him that I would refuse. But with typical resilience he recovered; grew a beard and tobacco (in the back garden), and indulged in all the slovenly habits that Mother would never allow: staying in bed till noon, not taking a bath (unless bullied by me), and not wearing a tie. Mother would have expected me to look after him. I compromised: I visited him three times a week.

During the summer he had had a couple of falls, one perilously near to the electric fire in his bedroom. But he made light of them: 'You'll have a shock when you come in one day and find me stretched out on the floor. But I shan't know anything about it.' His smile held more than a trace of malice.

He wouldn't let me stay with him. 'You have your own life to live. And I don't care when I go. You know that.'

A minor operation on his prostate gland; while still in hospital recovering, a major stroke followed by several minor ones left him apparently incontinent and helpless.

I could not understand what had happened. No one explained clearly. They talked vaguely about nature's healing powers. The truth I finally heard from the consultant neurologist: a rupture had occurred – inexplicably – in the membrane of his bladder. That was the reason for the incontinence. That was what they had been hoping for six months would heal itself. I suspected that someone's knife had slipped but no one was owning up. An operation would have been possible for a younger man but he would not be able to stand it. His condition was irreversible.

Finally, when they could do no more for him, fitted with a catheter and a urine bag he was sent home to die. I had promised that I would see him out – as he put it. He was my father and I loved him very much. What else could I do? Some thought one thing, some thought another. In the end I did the only thing I could do, I gave up my flat and moved in with him. It would not be for long, a couple of months at most, they said.

To be truthful it was also to my advantage I thought. Swings and roundabouts. I was tired of living in rented accommodation and tired of trying to keep my head above water financially, which was all it was, and tired of teaching. I could do with a breathing space, an opportunity to take stock and look around. (Had I known I would have run a mile.)

The small pathetic bundle of bones that the ambulance men deposited none too gently in his armchair by his fireside bore little resemblance to my father, the man who had walked into hospital six months earlier expecting to be there for a few days only. This old man looked permanently hunched and bent, staring witless eyes, mouth agape, nose with a drip on the end which he made no attempt to remove.

It was April and quite warm outside, but I had made a fire to take the chill off the atmosphere in the house and make it look welcoming. He didn't look round. He didn't utter a word. He seemed totally unaware of his surroundings.

What have I got myself into? My heart sank. I bolted for the kitchen and downed two sherries in swift succession with no noticeable effect.

When it came to putting him to bed, our concerted efforts could not move him. Fortunately it was Saturday, the builder's yard opposite was still open. The builder and one of his men carried him to bed. Mr Hurt, usually a placid man, looked very upset. 'I never thought to see Mr Hargreaves come to this.' They had been neighbours for twenty years. 'Anything I can do, any time, don't hesitate to ask.'

In the middle of the night my name, called desperately and repeatedly, woke me. Leaning on his walking frame outside his bedroom door, a comical figure: skinny little legs below a sopping wet nightshirt. A veritable Rumpelstiltskin, red-faced and furious. 'I've been calling and calling.'

'But Dad, it's the middle of the night.'

I changed him and helped him back to bed. Desperation had at least produced some mobility in him. As I turned to go a wistful voice said, 'But I'm still hungry.'

I realised that in the midst of everything I had absolutely forgotten to feed him. I apologised abjectly and made him some sandwiches and for the first time got a hint of a smile. I had not eaten anything either, but I had not felt hungry. I ate one of his sandwiches.

This was not the father I had known all my life. Any image I might have had of a loving father and daughter, of devotion and gratitude was swiftly forgotten. I was reminded of a cat we'd had when the children were small: a docile contented pet, good-tempered and placid. During a hot summer he had developed canine flu. To keep him away from the children we put him outside in the garden shed. In his attempts to get back into the house he became a spitting clawing spiteful bundle of hostility, not understanding our motives. But as soon as he was better and allowed inside again he reverted to his former sweetness of disposition.

Similarly Dad seemed to believe that everyone was against him, determined to deprive him of his autonomy, and I was the head jailer who enjoyed making him do what he didn't want to do. He resisted equally getting up in the morning and going to bed. He wouldn't move until the last note of the national anthem had been played on the TV.

I had acquired a cantankerous child. Unfortunately he wasn't going to get better. The situation wasn't helped by his conviction that he could look after himself. 'I'm not stopping you from going out. You go. I don't need a baby-sitter.'

'Not a babysitter. Someone to make you a cup of tea.'

His face reflected his hurt pride. 'I can do that.'

Behind his spectacles his eyes glared, his mouth worked fighting back the tears. I had to tell him that he couldn't. He couldn't even lift the kettle or negotiate the stairs down into the kitchen. He had to endure the same humiliation each time he was forced to recognise the truth of his condition.

'Why am I wearing this thing? Where's my dressing gown? This is a woman's. It was your mother's.'

'It's a man's dressing gown. If you remember Mother bought herself one like yours because it was so warm. Yours is wet.'

As soon as he was dry again he had no memory of ever being wet or any understanding of why he might be. The immediate past was gone irrevocably. He didn't know if he'd had his lunch; he didn't know where I was or how long I'd been gone, although I always told him exactly what was happening.

'Where have you been? Leaving me all alone. You've been gone for hours. You don't care what happens to me.' I had been away for five minutes, the time it took me to go to the end of the road and buy cigarettes.

Sometimes my patience would desert me and I would shout at him, 'I told you. I always tell you.'

His face crumpled, like a child when it has been scolded, 'Well I forget.' I felt mean.

He was constantly wet because he didn't drink enough to keep his urine clear and stop the catheter from clogging. But why should he believe me when he had no memory of it? 'If I drink too much it makes me want to pee.'

Is it nature's kindness that allows the old to forget their condition: the indignities, the humiliations? But he could still tell the district nurse, a novice gardener, how to grow roses and still quote large chunks of Shakespeare, especially his favourite, *Hamlet*, with feeling: 'O, that this too too solid flesh would melt; Thaw, and resolve itself into a dew . . .'

Two years later he was still alive and I was trapped.

That was the bitter pill. Hoist with my own petard. I meant to see him out with dignity and cold ham – another of his jokes. And somehow here I was again: my father flourishing – as far as an incontinent, forgetful old man can flourish – vainly trying to juggle my own needs against his.

His cheeks had filled out, his eyes were bright, his colour good: a loveable old man. In the morning he attempted the *Guardian* crossword and listened to Radio Three. In the afternoon his walking frame took him into the sitting-room to watch TV – he never forgot that!

I tried to make a life for myself. I went back to work and paid someone to come in and give him lunch. I went to evening classes. I joined a group: a T group, all the rage then, for the helping professions to learn the techniques of group management. In fact we all needed help ourselves and soon stopped pretending otherwise. And I fell in love, overwhelmingly, disastrously. I couldn't have picked anyone more unsuitable if I'd made a blueprint: very young, very married and riddled with guilt. Too much so even to be able to enjoy the 'brief encounter' that was all it ever really was, although it dragged its weary way on and off for four years, leaving me sadder but not any wiser – I was too angry, at him, at myself; mostly at myself who should have known better.

Two years later I went North again to stay with Jessica. Dad had gone into hospital for a couple of weeks to give me a break. But it wasn't enough. This time I was too tired to enjoy it. I returned as exhausted as when I left. I couldn't go on like this. I was making myself ill.

Home again I made arrangements for him to go into a nursing home, where he died a few weeks later.

I am at peace with my father's memory in a way that I am not with the memory of my mother. In old age she retreated behind a cloud of unreality to a place where I couldn't reach her. I felt cheated. I couldn't talk to her as I had been wont to do about the things that were important to me. We remained locked in a parent/child relationship. All that changed was who had the dependent role.

In every outward aspect my father had become unrecognisable. The quiet, easy-going good tempered man of few words who could always be relied on and was in charge of his life was gone. In his place a helpless invalid in control of nothing. But inside he remained the same man. That was why he was so cantankerous. He did not like what had happened to him and he was not going to pretend that he did. I wanted a little recognition for my sacrifice. Other people told me that he appreciated what I did. But that was the way of our family: feelings buttoned up, unacknowledged, good behaviour expected, taken for granted. He made nothing easy for me. He didn't want to go into a home. Why should he? I was forced to put it bluntly.

'It's your life or mine. I can't go on like this. I'm tired all the time, too tired even to enjoy a holiday. Dr Taylor says I shall be ill if I go on. And then I wouldn't be able to look after you anyway. It's no life.'

He was quiet for a long time. At first he hadn't taken me seriously. How could he know how much attention I had to give him? He couldn't believe that I was really expecting him to leave his home. When his back was to the wall his mind was as sharp as ever. He was fighting for his life. His cheeks were flushed a dull patchy red. His eyes were full of unshed tears. But finally he saw that I meant it.

'So it's you or me. That's what you're saying.'

'Yes. I'm sorry.'

'If you put it like that – I don't want to spoil your life – I'll go.'

I had already asked the local authority if they could help. I couldn't afford a private nurse.

'Your father needs professional nursing,' the health visitor told me. 'We have no provision for that.' She looked puzzled when I pointed out that I was not a professional nurse, but no one objected to me looking after him. 'That's different. You're his daughter. And I can see that he's very well cared for. If you saw some of the people that I am responsible for . . .'

Relatives, especially daughters, are in a special category. There's no limit to what they can do.

The nursing home was very comfortable, more like a large country house than an institution: traditional carpets, brasses in the reception hall and flowers, dark oak furniture, comfortable armchairs in the bright sitting-room, pleasant chintz covers and curtains; a young and friendly staff and an informal atmosphere. It was the matron's life as well her job, and her home. She genuinely cared for all her charges. But my father metaphorically turned his face to the wall. He wouldn't eat, he wouldn't talk, he wouldn't join the others in the communal sitting-room.

'What have I got in common with a lot of people who are either stupid or like zombies?' There was something in what he said.

They gave him his own TV. He didn't even turn it on. He sat staring at nothing.

'He looks like a man with a secret sorrow,' the matron said. 'But he never complains.'

'He is a very determined man. I think he has decided to die.'

When I asked him what was the matter and if he wanted to come home again he said he was fine. At the time I was angry with him. I felt he was punishing me. But now I can see that he was doing what he always did: exercising his autonomy, in so far as he was able, in whatever circumstances he found himself. If he couldn't live in his own home then he didn't want to live at all.

Someone in my group suggested that he had done it for me. A gift. But I wanted him to live and be happy, or at least let me be happy for a while. The relief when I left him in the nursing home was enormous. I didn't want him to die.

He had a photograph of my mother as a young woman on his bedside table. Sometimes he talked about their early days together: how beautiful she was, though she didn't know it: so vivid like a flame, so alive, like quicksilver; how happy they had been.

I was getting ready to go and see him on a Sunday morning

at the end of March when the matron rang. He'd had a stroke while being offered and refusing his breakfast as usual and was now in a deep coma. The doctor did not expect him to recover. He could go at any time.

Spring was firmly established for the first time that year, even in the suburban streets on the way to the nursing home: in the faint but aspiring sunshine, the trees delicately greening, and the clouds of dusty pink and white blossom that stand so stark and beautiful against the bare black branches of the thorn tree and bring a lift to the heart as the first signal that winter is truly over. It is strange how alive everything seems and how aware of it one is when someone is dying.

My father had fallen asleep. He looked so peaceful, all lines smoothed out of his face, a faint colour in his cheeks, a slight breath stirring his parted lips. He lay on his side with one hand under his cheek as he often did when asleep. But this was the sleep of death. He would not awake. Nor did I want him to. It was his choice. He died early next morning.

Now he is dead. And I am guilty of his death. He would still be alive if I had kept him at home. His only surviving sister died shortly before he did. I have run out of elderly relatives to be needed by. Now I can get on with my life, can't I?

I go back to work although the GP offers me more time off. But I can't stay away for ever, I have to get back in there eventually.

Now there's nothing between me and 'life'.

I tell myself that I want to join in.

I clean the house. I throw out a lot of old junk. My parents had never thrown away so much as a bus ticket. I scour away the smell of urine and dirt and old people. I move things around to make the house my own. But I don't fool myself; it makes little difference.

I sit in my clean house and listen to the silence.

I am like a little girl who's got herself dressed up for a party. The house is clean and shining. The table is laid with sandwiches and jelly and cake. But no one comes. Has she got the day wrong? Has she forgotten to send out the invitations? Or do they simply not like her?

When I was young I hated parties, especially my own; agonies of embarrassment, dressed up like a dog's dinner in a frilly dress. Too-hot rooms and games in which someone was made to look silly while everyone else laughed, and having to join in and pretend I liked it. As I grew older I avoided this by volunteering to help in the kitchen.

Someone once described me to my mother as the sort of girl who would always be there with a bucket if a bucket was what was wanted, without waiting to be asked. That was considered a great compliment.

What do you do when nobody wants a bucket? I'm tired. I wonder what it has all been for, the struggle to change, the years of analysis, of trying to understand?

ii

I had often wondered what a breakdown would be like, what it would mean to break down: totally letting go, of responsibility, of control. Curious and half envious; I had bent, I had cracked, but I had never broken; I couldn't imagine it.

My earlier descent into the abyss had been in many ways quite controlled, something I did when there was nothing more pressing and I had the time. I was at the same time managing a house and a family (not very efficiently), helping to look after my mother and teaching part-time.

This time the descent was sudden, completely unexpected and involuntary. No warning, no idea of what was going to happen until it did and by then it was already too late.

I thought I was managing very well: keeping going, filling my place at work, going through the motions. In between classes I sat at my desk with a book open in front of me, a pen in my hand in case anyone should come in, and looked out of the window, my mind a blank. At night I fell asleep sitting up, often with the light on and my glasses on. If I lay down there was a roaring in my head and a pounding in my ears and my chest. Lifting my father had damaged my back. It was very painful. Pills killed the pain but left my muscles limp and useless.

A year after his death my younger daughter, Lottie, the final person that I thought still might need me, went abroad with a friend. She intended to stay at least six months, longer if she liked it. She had got herself a work-permit and a job, so there was no urgency to return.

The morning after she left I couldn't get myself ready for work. I couldn't move out of my chair. I put it down to my back and thought I would be better the next day. I rang Myrtle, for whom I had sometimes done the same, to ask her to look after my pupils, just for today. By mistake the switchboard put me through to Douglas, the senior psychologist, and I heard myself telling him that I couldn't get into work. He was very sympathetic, told me to take a few days off and go to see my doctor.

To my GP, Dr Taylor, I said. 'I don't know what's the matter with me,' and burst into tears. Quite out of character. I usually have my diagnosis ready.

'What's happened?'

'Lottie's gone.' It slipped out unbidden. 'That sounds awful, I want her to go.'

'Of course you do.'

He told me I was depressed and to come and see him again in two weeks. Anything else he expected Dr Penny and I could take care of.

I shall be back soon I assured everyone, and myself.

Days slid into weeks, weeks into months. It was as if Dr

Taylor had given me permission and I went home and fell to pieces. I had been right when I thought that if I stopped I wouldn't be able to start again. I had given up the unequal struggle. I couldn't move, I couldn't do anything. And I couldn't think of any reason why I should. I couldn't talk and I couldn't eat.

My head was full of cotton wool. Thought was elusive. I had forgotten the beginning of a sentence before I reached the end. The noise in my head was complete, cutting me off from everything and everyone. I slept only an hour or so at a time. Falling asleep was an abrupt and vertiginous descent into a strange surrealist underworld of weird, evanescent, constantly changing shapes. Half-glimpsed ugly creatures of menacing aspect followed me or lurked around corners waiting. I wandered through a landscape in which nothing could be positively identified; nothing was clearly visible; everything was distorted and bathed in lurid swirling kaleidoscopic colours: harsh glowing reds, acidic greens, virulent blues. Exhausted I dragged myself up and out of that abominable place. It was preferable to be awake. Marginally so because the nightmare world had broken through into my waking life: strange visions, hypnagogic images superimposed themselves on my sight: heraldic beasts, mythical monsters, ancient designs like those on an Egyptian scroll replaced the wallpaper in my bedroom, obscured the pink rosebuds Mother had chosen, and danced across the mirror of the rickety old oak dressing table in majestic procession. At the edge of my vision small birds and animals darted and flittered.

Sleeping pills made no difference except that falling asleep was more immediate and deeper, and the waking more difficult though just as soon. Sedation only increased the nightmare effect. But awake I could touch familiar, solid things like tables and chairs. I could move around, put the kettle on, make a cup of tea.

Time was marked by changes in the light, and appointments with Dr P which somehow I managed to keep. Friends, colleagues came to visit, brought tempting snacks I didn't eat and gossip I wasn't interested in. From the beginning they urged me to come back to work. It was bad for me to sit at home doing nothing, 'vegetating, dwelling on morbid thoughts, getting more depressed'. I needed taking out of myself. That puzzled me, it was the wrong way round. I wanted to say to them: I can't work because I'm ill. When I'm better I shall be able to and then I will come back to work. That's the right way round. But I didn't, I couldn't formulate it, I couldn't say anything. I didn't talk to them and soon they stopped coming, all except one who had not given me any advice. She continued to come nearly every day on her way home, with a flask of soup that I didn't eat. But I was glad she came. And glad in a remote way that any of them took the trouble to.

Hollyhocks by the fence in the front garden grew tall and leaned across the gate where they met drooping branches from the buddleia tree. Myrtle complained that it was as difficult to find a way in to see me as to the Sleeping Beauty. I apologised but secretly I was pleased. Let it be difficult. Let it be like that for a hundred years. Prince Charming wasn't coming and no one else need bother.

Lack of sleep, lack of food and exercise led me on a downwardly spiralling path. This was now my routine. At whatever time I rose – it might be as early as four a.m., glad to be rid of the night – I sat in my father's wooden armchair (its straight back was good for my spine), a long skirt and a loose jumper over my nightclothes, outwardly neat and composed. On my right the living-room window looked out on to an expanse of cracked concrete and a rickety wooden fence. No flowers, only a few spindly weeds forcing their way through the cracks. This dilapidated view pleased me, suited me especially in the grey light of early morning. Under the window stood the table that had housed Mother's sewing machine until arthritis made it too painful for her to use and she passed it on to my sister-in-law. Now it held my record player. I could change the records without moving. At my elbow on the old scrubbed wooden kitchen table (a relic of childhood), coffee and cigarettes: all I needed. I played the same few records over and over: Alan Price, songs of his childhood, memories of the Jarrow hunger march; a Gaelic folk lament; Dory Previn, *Reflections in a Mud Puddle*, about her childhood; and the piano rags of Scott Joplin. I liked the wit and the anger of Price and Previn, the underlying melancholy of Scott Joplin. The music was comforting, speaking to me directly in a language without need of words. In the afternoon, TV soaps put me to sleep for an hour or so. I only ever saw the first few minutes.

So it continued. I wasn't living, I wasn't dying – though I suspected that if I went on like this for long I might. Sitting in my father's chair one day feeling weak and faint, I thought, if I don't move I shall die. It was my first coherent thought. And I got up and walked across the room and felt the blood begin to circulate through my hands and feet, tingling and hurting. So I wasn't ready to die yet. Not like that, just sitting there, not without a fight. But I didn't want to live either. A paradox my mind couldn't begin to grapple with.

Dr P was in charge. For that I was grateful. My condition had to be ratified by a psychiatrist, which she was. I also had to be declared fit again, mentally and emotionally, before I would be allowed to resume teaching. Fair enough. But it reminded me uneasily of horror stories I had heard about people unjustly placed in mental hospitals, sometimes for years – easier to get in than out, once labelled. Dr P spared me that ordeal. Dr Taylor declared his ignorance of mental and emotional processes, carefully guarded himself in fact from any attempt on my part to enlighten him, and was happy to leave 'all that' to her.

This caused a strange shift in our relationship, one I don't think she was very happy about. One thing for me to fantasise about being totally dependent on her, but now in reality I was, in one respect at least. Her way of dealing with this was to involve me in the process, keeping me informed and consulting me about every decision she had to make, every letter she wrote on my behalf. I hated the thought of having to be examined by a strange psychiatrist who knew nothing about me and certainly wouldn't share either his thoughts or his decisions with me. Dr P. while acting as a buffer between me and the authorities, kept me in touch with reality, making me take responsibility for myself. I didn't like it, though I expect it was necessary. But I was tired of being responsible. Where had it ever got me? Yet I suspect that I would have been very upset if she hadn't consulted me!

*

It was a fine spring that year. The gradually warming sun mocked my seclusion.

Jessica came for the weekend and sat me outside in the garden on what, once a lawn, was now more like a meadow, with a rug round my knees. The sporadic forays I'd made on the garden while Dad was alive had been swallowed up. Nature was reclaiming her territory. Blackberry bushes from the bottom of the garden spread prickly octopus tentacles everywhere. Convolvulus festooned the fence and was gaining a stranglehold on the climbing roses. But spring was late and growth still subdued. The early comers, fresh young blades of grass and purple-shaded bluebells, spread a magic carpet overall, blurring my vision with nostalgic tears. Black-birds and thrushes sang loudly and competitively; even some-where a cuckoo called.

But by July bad weather had set in again.

Jessica hired a Caravette, a combination small car and caravan, and bundled me, a few warm clothes and a sleeping bag into the back, and with Jonah we set off for a tour of the Western Highlands. It made no difference to me where I was as long as no effort was demanded of me.

It was dark and inevitably raining when we finally stopped

for the night. In a glen, Jessica said. There was nothing to be seen but rain slanting across the headlights and a few wet bushes in the circle of light. But the distant sound of rushing water gave credence to her confident statement.

In my sleeping bag curled comfortably around her sleeping form I lay and listened to the astonishing silence. The rain had stopped except for the occasional spatter of drops blown from the trees on to our roof. My ears filled with the sound of water running, rushing, gurgling, splashing, drowning out all other sounds, obliterating the noises in my head as nothing else had been able to. I fell asleep soothed by its many voices, peace stealing over me.

I woke after an unprecedented number of hours' sleep. It was very strange to be lying relaxed and comfortable and warm. Through steamed-up windows vague shapes, humps of distant hills. Nearer at hand the sound of water dominating everything. I drank it in like a thirsty traveller arrived at an oasis. For ten days it rained. We saw Scotland through a mist of rain; leaves blown on the wind, black hillsides splashed with foaming white cascades: waterfalls in full spate. At night when the rain ceased the sky was full of brilliant stars, coming down so low over the hills it seemed we could almost reach up and touch them. The moon was reflected in silvery gleams on the wet grass and pools on the tarmacked road. And for ten days I was happy.

If we could have gone on and on, carried around in a motorised cradle, lulled to sleep every night by the music of the wind and the waters, warmed by the proximity of non-threatening bodies, friendly and protective, I knew I would soon be better. A world apart; a world without care; of wild dawns and blood-red sunsets; a beautiful world as it must have been at the beginning; sleeping and waking at the foot of forest-covered hills beside vast expanses of water with only the birds for company.

Hill and glen, dark and light, turbulent streams, mirror-glass lakes: ever changing, ever the same: God's world not mine. 'Thine is the kingdom, the power and the glory, for ever and ever.' The words made a refrain in my head.

Diminished to my proper status, healed or broken, maimed or whole, like an unravelled garment I was being knitted up again. This was what I needed: life at its most basic, and I at my most irresponsible.

Jessica pleased herself. She loved driving; she loved Scotland. Each morning, 'ready or not', she set off. I sat in the back in my sleeping bag, bleary-eyed, peering out at the world like a disgruntled caterpillar raising its head, unwashed and uncombed. The occasional passing labourer was startled by the sight of my wildly flailing arms as I struggled to disentangle myself and drag on some clothes in a fast-moving vehicle.

Only the very young, the very old or the very rich can lay claim to the kind of devoted attention that I wanted. Even then I doubt if it is ever exactly right. For ten days it was. Bowling along in our little mobile home there was no clash of interest. My needs were few: cigarettes, tea and coffee, and to be left alone. My daughters had become experts at that. They were used to my moods. We had an unspoken mutual agreement. They were not concerned to improve me or make me better, nor I them. They had had to live through a lot of unpleasantness during the break-up of the marriage, and had both supported me at a time when it should have been the other way round. They had their own difficulties, for which I felt responsible, and was.

Jonah was immersed in his own thoughts and feelings. His mother had died recently. Whenever we stopped he made for the nearest hilltop and stayed there until it was time to move on. In between times we all enjoyed the carefree sensation of doing as we liked (none of us was very good at that): we argued amicably, played childish games and sang as we drove along, competing fiercely about things that didn't matter at all. On this holiday I felt the first stirrings of hunger. Enticing smells in the restaurants they dragged me into and their healthy appetites got my taste buds going. I had to go with them or face the darkness alone. But my stomach seemed to have shrunk; the first mouthfuls tasted like straw and I ate little. In spite of that the packets of Complan, recommended by Dr P when she discovered I wasn't eating, returned home unopened.

But idylls are of necessity short-lived.

Home again I sank back into apathy and despair and sleepless nights. The last two weeks had been a respite: time out. But the memory of it sustained me.

I was living so near the bone, my nerve endings so exposed to every impression that the surface of things, the trappings, the decorations that help to make life pleasant were seen only as what they sometimes are: a tawdry covering like plastic gift-wrapping, a mask hiding the ugly face of reality. I could see the raw bones under plump flesh, the corruption at the heart of beauty, the fixed grimace of death behind every smile. But the natural world in all its variety: that world accepted me as I was. I couldn't live there. Too much a city dweller I'm afraid of the dark, lost without streets and shops and artificial light. But in my bones I recognise it as the right and proper place, the home of my ancestors.

iii

The return to health was slow. My lodgers had married and gone. I didn't replace them. I was alone as I had always known I would be one day. I drifted through the empty rooms like a ghost dimly reflected in the tarnished dusty mirrors, pale and gaunt, at home in the shadows.

When I was young I had five maiden aunts: independent women who carved out careers for themselves. When they came to stay they brought me splendid extravagant presents. They had provided many of my best-loved dolls. But although they wore smarter clothes and were more affluent than my mother I knew there was something wrong about them. Compared to her they were second-class citizens, failed in the great test of womanhood: husbandless and child-less. And, as respectable women of their time, I assumed also sex-less.

That was not going to be me. As a five-year-old I said firmly, 'I'm going to be a teacher like Mummy and marry a man like Daddy.' I knew already I couldn't have Daddy.

But here I was now. This woman in the mirror was she any better than they, was she in fact half as good? They had made themselves a life, the best they could in the circum-stances. If they sometimes dewed their lonely pillow with tears nobody knew.

Aunt Maria, who lived with us and was the object of my dubious pity, told me on her deathbed that she had had a very happy life. Perhaps she had and I was too stupid to see it. It was in the eyes of society, including Mother's and my own, that she was found wanting. A verdict I accepted with facile condescension. Aunt Maria had been a lady's maid. With her aristocratic employer she learned court dressmaking and fine embroidery and all the etiquette of refined living that my brother and I used to scoff at. She travelled abroad and learned foreign languages. When the Great War put a stop to her travels she went into a munitions factory and helped the war effort. In her spare time she learned carpentry, a skill she used to make cupboards and a wardrobe and even a folding bed in her flat at the top of our house. After the war she joined the Civil Service and became a youth employment officer for girls. She never lost her adventurous spirit. When she retired from work she went to be matron at a hostel full of Spanish children, refugees from the Spanish Civil War. They called her Aunty and loved her dearly and when she died from a heart attack, having disobeyed the doctor's orders and climbed a hill to take back the clothes she had mended for them, they all attended her funeral and brightened the church with arms full of daffodils. (You can see how easy it was for me to feel superior. For of course she never married.) In her day she was quite a beauty. She wrote in letters to her favourite sister, my mother, of stealing out late at night in Venice, Florence and Rome to keep secret assignations with young Italian aristocrats, having thoughtfully locked her elderly employer in her bedroom first. Among her effects Mother and I found a locket with a photo of a melancholy man with drooping moustaches. His name was Wilfred. They had been in love, Mother said, but as she was the sole support of his mother and several sisters he could never afford to marry.

She was a very reserved woman, but she took me to the theatre, the ballet and to my first art exhibition. I wish I had been able to know her better.

Now, however, I am trying to look at myself and others more clearly.

I didn't understand what was happening to me. Kind friends took me for drives and pub lunches in pleasant country lanes. I still got 'pull yourself together' admonitions from some. I enjoyed the drives and ignored the advice. I didn't attempt to argue. But everything in me was one gigantic no: at first helplessly so, and then as the feelings gathered strength more deliberately. When they talked of food I lost my appetite, when they talked of work and making an effort I drowned in waves of exhaustion. I couldn't explain, they didn't understand. I had nothing to say to them. Had I ever had, except as a form of politeness? They exhorted me not to give in, not to let myself become a vegetable. I couldn't tell them how lively things were inside my head. It would only have alarmed them.

I had worked hard, I had tried. And so what?

As usual when I don't understand I asked Dr P, 'Do you have any idea what's going on? I don't.'

She said, 'I think you are wanting to go back to the beginning and start again, and this time do it differently.'

That made sense. Everything I had done so far had ended

in failure. Why should I go on like that? I would rather die. Of one thing I was sure: for the rest of my life – that rapidly dwindling commodity – I was not going to look after anyone but myself. Giving would come way behind getting. But old habits die hard. How do you change? Talking is easy. Dr P and I had done that endlessly.

When coherent thought returned, that seemed to be what my breakdown was about: 'I can't get it right, so I'm not going to keep on trying. I shall sit here until I see some point, or until I die. Whichever comes first.'

I'm putting into words now as I couldn't then, the sense of my determined obstinacy, of my utter despair and my absolute refusal to do what 'they' wanted.

*

I had been summoned by letter to a review of my case by an independent psychiatrist, the chief health officer of the county. It was six months since I had stopped working. They wanted to know if I was swinging the lead. They didn't put it like that though.

A friend dropped me at the door and would pick me up again later, but was too busy to stay with me as I would have liked. It was only a fifteen-minute journey by car but it felt like the outer reaches of space, so alone and friendless did I feel. Outwardly calm I sat smoking one cigarette after another in a dingy waiting room, unpleasantly reminiscent of waiting for punishment outside the headmistress's room (it was an old condemned school), and admired the performance of the only other candidate. She looked very young and so did her husband and brother who were trying vainly to comfort her. She walked up and down unsteadily on her platform soles and gasped for breath and cried and wailed that she couldn't stand it, she should never have come, she'd have to go. They held on to her and agreed with her, murmuring placatingly, but now you're here . . . Fortunately for all of us she was seen first. I felt increasingly sane and normal, and wondered what I was doing there.

Her cries sounded faintly through the wall, and then silence. She returned indignant but subdued. On a rising crescendo of outrage she said, 'He says I'm better. He says, if I'm well enough to complain I'm well enough for work. He says I'm all right. Old fool!' lowering her voice.

'He wouldn't say that if he had to live with you,' muttered her husband.

'Never mind, eh?' said her brother philosophically. My heart sank. What chance had I?

To my surprise the 'old fool' was quite pleasant. He asked me to describe how I felt: take your time, no hurry. I could hear my voice, flat, unemotional. It was as if I was two people: one watching the other perform, seeing the sympathy in the unguarded face of the nurse who sat behind him, thinking, you're doing a great job; admiring my performance, feeling a charlatan: the other cowering, quite desperate, dreading the judgement of a stranger.

When I stopped talking he glanced through some papers in front of him and said, 'Your doctor's account agrees with yours. He's written a very good report. He thinks you need time and that the best person to help you is your analyst. I agree with him. I shall simply endorse his recommendations. I wish everyone made my job so easy.' He shook my hand. 'I hope you soon begin to feel better.'

Reprieve. Permission. And from a stranger, who believed me, or anyway my GP (dear Dr T), who didn't judge me harshly, in fact didn't judge me at all.

The second summer after I stopped working I went to stay with Lottie in Toronto.

My first flight. The idea terrified me. I had said I would never fly unless one of my children needed me. Now Lottie was making me prove my words. Though the question of who needed who was moot. Fortunately Jonah was going too. I held his hand and wept and believed I was going to die and marvelled at the sight of 'paradise' above the clouds: the pure untainted blue, the rosy-peaked cloud masses; and thought it might be worth dying to have seen it. I was in a painting by Salvador Dali or a strange space odyssey, hurtling through time and space in a silver bullet to the strains of Roses of the South on my headphones. Finally coming down out of the clouds to Toronto airport and 'safety', knowing Lottie was waiting for me. A faith not even disturbed by the sardonic voice of Jonah in my ear, 'This is the most dangerous bit.'

Five weeks of hot, humid weather and blazing sun, such as I had never experienced; sometimes only able to lie on my bed and sweat until the sun went down.

Lottie had a small apartment in a rooming house out in the leafy suburbs: one L-shaped room, a washroom and a verandah overlooking the street. Jonah stayed for a few days, sleeping on the floor, and then went on to Montreal.

Invisible but all-seeing on the verandah set back under the eaves, I sat and watched all day while Lottie was at work: the wide unfenced grass verges, the wood-framed houses reminiscent of the thirties, the loud-voiced friendly people, the screaming of brakes as the young men hurled their large cars aggressively round the corner; the feeling of space, of trees having enough room to grow to their full height and spread their branches; instead of pollarded plane trees, the red maple and the red squirrel.

We did all the touristy things: ate hot dogs, dined at a drive-in restaurant, went to a drive-in movie, swooshed to the top of the observation tower, leaving my stomach at the bottom to be collected, loitered on Main Street – disappointingly small and tame – and the crowning glory, a visit to the second-rate nightclub where Lottie's boyfriend was a temporary waiter. Small and a little shabby it was patronised by middle-aged working men and women out for a good time and the refurbishing of their dreams. The women had bouffant hair styles, the 'beehives' of an earlier era, too much make-up and dresses a little too young and too tight for them. The men, loud check shirts, cowboy hats and high boots, red faces and beer bellies. They drank too much and became maudlin and a little quarrelsome and sang with much feeling the old Country and Western songs. For *Stand by Your Man* they rose as one and sang with as much fervour as for the national anthem, tears rolling down their cheeks.

At ease with Lottie as if we had only left each other the day before, it was another cocooned existence. If I could stay here in this pleasant place, participating in her life vicariously but not seriously involved on my own behalf, everything would be fine. Lottie was enjoying her new life with her new love, and expanding in it. She could include me in without strain, for a while. Other people's lives I could manage, it was my own I couldn't cope with. I despised my inability just to get on with it. Other people thought life desirable. Did they really believe that? Or were they pretending too? I'm making it sound as if I think other people have it easy, as if for instance it hadn't been difficult for Lottie alone in a strange country without family or friends. But the truth was: for once in my life I was more concerned about myself than anyone else. That sounds selfish. It is. Or is it just common sense?

Whatever, sooner or later, lovely daughters notwithstanding, I had to be on my own. This wasn't a fight I wanted, it was a fight I had to have, had been landed with – no choice, not even take it or leave it.

*

September: the school year beginning.

Worn down by the barrage of exhortation and well-intentioned advice I learned cunning. I couldn't afford to listen to them. I had been listening to them or someone just like them all my life. But I could not afford to alienate them either, especially those like the psychologists, with influence in the education office. There must be no suspicion of malingering.

One day I would want a job to return to. I had to act on that assumption, though I couldn't imagine it. No doubt they were worried about me, and sincerely believed they were acting in my best interests. If I let myself go, if I didn't make an effort, I would become totally demoralised, would never be able to pick myself up again: so they believed. I felt harassed and persecuted. (And partly was afraid that they were right. Shades of Mother. How did I know?) But I had no energy to argue. Now I was listening to myself. Finally I discovered a simple formula. If I smiled they thought I was better, and a joke, which I will probably be telling on my deathbed, was evidence of complete recovery. On the other hand if I was gloomy and taciturn – oh dear you're still no better, they said – they left me alone. So I learned how to keep them out of my hair. Just don't smile!

To show goodwill, I did go to work one autumn morning, 'Just to see how you get on.' No schoolboy more unwilling. As soon as I closed the heavy doors behind me and began to climb the echoing stone steps towards the Remedial Unit I felt dizzy and faint. Old schools have an unmistakable smell, a damp chilly smell, compound of sweaty feet and chalk dust and places where the sun never shines. There were bright smiles in welcome and an unimportant filing job to make me feel useful. When the walls began to close in I left abruptly. They couldn't say I hadn't tried.

My only other appearance was at the end–of–term party. They had put on such a spread with china and wine glasses and the tablecloth I had once given the unit and flowers, and they looked so pleased to see me that I burst into tears. I completed my performance of a 'woman having a break- down' by spilling coffee all over the chief psychologist, the one I called the friendly dragon, and dropping my cup at her feet. She mopped us both up with unruffled calm. I could see that they did care, even though I couldn't respond.

And now I see more than I could afford to then how hard they worked to keep the way open for me to come back to work.

As in a dream another year passed.

No doubt about it, I was better. I looked better, I felt better. But not better enough for work, as far as I was concerned. I would have liked to stop altogether but I couldn't afford to. I had no other source of income. Periodically the Department of Education sent letters to Dr P asking if I was fit to return to work. A new school year was imminent. Logically a good time to make a new start. She said she thought I should. She thought I was fit enough and I had to start sometime. The longer I put it off the more difficult.

Extract from a letter to Lottie:

> Convinced I'm doing the right thing. Haven't been into work at all this week. It isn't easy being alone fighting myself, but that's where it is.
>
> Dr P isn't convinced. She thinks I can't go to work because I put the judgement of being a good girl on to it. If I didn't I could work, and work through the feelings as well. She's wrong. It's the good girl that makes me go at all. I don't want to. Nothing to give any other child but me. When I can give myself things I may be able to give to other people. But not yet. Also she underestimates my physical tiredness. Three days to put the sitting-room straight after the carpet was laid. Usually three hours. I'm not living a 'normal' life. I don't go anywhere except to her. I see a lot of people but they all have to come to see me. When I'm out I want to be at home all the time.
>
> She says, 'Doesn't the time drag?' And that's the point, it doesn't. It isn't very pleasant. But there still isn't enough time for all I want to do. I'm not bored, more tormented. And in between, just tired. I still don't sleep much.

Shall have to continue the argument. That's what it's about – how I see things, not how she does.

Found myself saying to her this morning, 'No, no, no, no, no.'

She had gone over to the enemy. I was desperate. Everyone else was at me to come back. If she deserted me I was sunk. I spent an uncomfortable few days. A decision had to be made. When I took my head out of the sand and faced what I'd been avoiding: the idea, the fact of returning to work, I was conscious of an overwhelming sense of disappointment. It rose from the depths taking me by surprise, and wouldn't go away. Logically they and she were right. I had to start sometime. Why not now? I could manage. But everything in me cried out against it.

I had never thought of myself as a delicate child. I don't suppose Mother would have allowed me to. But I remembered recurring bouts of bronchitis, fires in my bedroom, steaming kettles and friar's balsam and a slow recovery. Also 'bilious' attacks, so-called, attributed to my liver, something I ate, or getting over-excited. I was laid out for one or two days. They seemed to occur whenever something good was in the offing like an outing or a holiday. The rest of the family would depart and Mother and I would stay behind until I was better, so as well as feeling ill I felt guilty at spoiling things for her. Not that she ever complained.

But the main thing I remember is having to get up before I felt well enough. Mother firmly believed, and so therefore did I, that to stay in bed one day more than was absolutely necessary would be the first step on the slippery downward slope. Eternal vigilance was needed to keep the forces of moral degradation at bay. I found this easy to believe because to begin with Mother was always right, and I did feel that I never wanted to get up again at the point at which I had to. Self-indulgence and over-indulgence must always be avoided, and being ill came into both those categories.

'Always get up from the table feeling you could eat a little more' – Mother quoting from Malcolm Sargent, the famous conductor. Look where abstemiousness got him! When he later died from cancer I felt cheated and inwardly sure he must have fallen from grace – too many cream buns no doubt.

Father was in this, as in everything else, exempt from Mother's rules. He ate until he was full and then slept it off. If he got a cold he went to bed and stayed there until it was better – unlike the rest of us, who staggered around bravely. But he was rarely ill and his behaviour was always beyond criticism.

Now I was in revolt against all those years of Mother's rule and never, even when supposedly independent and running my own household, being able to decide for myself how I felt and what to do. I had lived all my life by those rules, so deeply engrained that they had become like my conscience, and as a self-fulfilling prophesy they ensured that I would suffer if I broke them.

Now Dr P was telling me what to do. Could I not for once make my own decisions? Couldn't I be trusted to know what was best for me? I see now that the person I had to convince was myself. But at the time I felt intolerably pressured. Mother was on my back again – as she often was in my dreams. I explained all this to Dr P. Fortunately she understood and wrote to the Department of Education that I needed a little more time; it would be unwise for me to return to work prematurely. They granted me a further three months' sick leave, unpaid. That made a total of twenty months.

Unfortunately my relief was clouded by guilt. No one would believe I wasn't pulling a fast one.

One damp October morning I rushed out to the dustbin in my bedroom slippers and skidded, falling full length and cracking my head open on the stone step. In a state of shock I walked to the casualty department of the local hospital – gathering some curious stares on the way – where they cleaned me up and sewed up the gash. The result was quite spectacular: a livid gash, a swollen nose and black eyes, gaining me a lot of undeserved sympathy. No one mentioned work and I was convinced I had done it on purpose. It looked much worse than it felt.

What had begun involuntarily as a vacant stare sitting in a chair unable to move, over the months had become a deliberate turning inwards to commune with myself, a necessary meditation, reflecting and taking stock. Looking outwards, in books and to other people for answers, I had found none. I suffered from a fever with no medical cure, a hunger and a need for which there is no material palliative. My GP offered me anti-depressants. I had taken them after my marriage broke up for a while and they had enabled me to carry on, dampened down unbearable feelings and made them manageable. But for the real problem central to my very existence they offered no solution. Little of this showed on the outside. How could I expect people to understand? If I didn't why should they, unless they had been through something similar?

Shortly before Christmas my ultimate boss, the chief education officer of the local authority, issued an ultimatum. If I didn't return to work in January they could not guarantee to keep my position open for me any longer. Events were bringing their own kind of pressure to bear. In a climate of recession I would find it difficult to get another job. Part-time teachers, always the first to feel the pinch, were already being laid off. How could I with my well-blotted copybook hope to compete? This was different from my battle with Dr P. That had been about my right to self-determination. The education committee owed me nothing. They had been more than generous already. But their concern was for the education service as a whole, not for one cog in it. Facts of life are inconvenient but impersonal, and don't hurt nearly as much as more personal transactions. The decision was still mine. Reluctantly I agreed to go back to work at the beginning of the next school term, in January.

How I wished for the intervention of a *deus ex machina*. Something, a broken leg, anything that would stop me, without it being my fault. But fate did not intervene. I dragged my unwilling feet step by step to the classroom door without hindrance.

And so it began again – learning how to survive, how to get by, how to live. This time with a different emphasis. This time it was for me.

*

At last I realise that I have only one life. Not tomorrow, not some time in the future but now. I've always behaved as if life were a 'coming attraction', like the cinema. One day I'll get around to it and it'll be great. A film can come round again. Life won't, not this one anyway. One day it will be too late. Today has gone by unheeded. Tomorrow never comes. In the army, my father said, they were always promised jam tomorrow. Which meant they never got it.

I knew I had changed. But the longer we worked the stronger was the feeling of connection with the child I had been. And the more it felt as if I was reverting to a former self. A self I had despised as stupid, had been told was over-emotional and over-sensitive, thought of as naïve and sentimental and having unreal expectations. She wanted to be a dancer, a singer, a writer. But her talent was small, her energy less. But it was she, the lost child who gave back meaning to my life, a continuity of purpose like a thread that steadily unreels from birth to death.

I had hoped to find a newer, better, finer me. Instead I found the old despised one: the passionate, sad, lonely child, the dancer, the singer, the poet.

But what I had acquired remained too: the questioning

self-doubt, the cynical distrust (which I called realism). And with reason. People are made uneasy if you change and may put obstacles in your way. They fear it will be demanded of them next.

At the Centre for Transpersonal Psychology I heard the mid-life crisis described as an 'opportunity to break down in order to break through'. That is an apt if cursory summary of what happened to me. And continued to happen. It doesn't end as suddenly as it begins unfortunately. I had moved the venue is all. Come out of hiding. Now a different, in some ways harder struggle begins because others are watching. Some helping, some not.

One of the favourite stories of my childhood was *The Bluebird* by Maurice Maeterlink, in which two children search for the bluebird of happiness. After many journeys and adventures they return home without it only to discover that it has been at home all the time. This idea, perhaps wrongly interpreted, appealed to my timidity and was encouraged by Mother: if it's here no need to look elsewhere. Forgetting the importance of the journey itself, and that finding out where things are *not* may be as important, may in fact be necessary, before you can find out where they are.

Everything contains and is defined by its opposite. As Dr P said, 'How can you recognise Heaven if you have no experience of Hell?' In the grey monotony my life had become I experienced neither.

Persistent images showed where the recalcitrant aspects of my being lingered or mal-lingered, obstinately impervious to demands for change. There were no short cuts. I came to understand what Jung meant when he said 'through not round'.

iv

It was not the job I'd left: the same building, but not the same people. The psychologists and social workers had gone elsewhere. We were all teachers. I didn't know any of them, nor did I want to. Which made it difficult all round. They looked at me sideways waiting for me to foam at the mouth or do something peculiar; half frightened, half hoping. I felt exposed and vulnerable. If I made a joke no one laughed. Mad people don't have a sense of humour. I didn't want to be there. But that wasn't their fault. They didn't know how to treat me and I didn't make it easy. Wrestling with inner demons tends to impose a grim and unrelenting aspect on the face. I didn't smile much. And I must admit my jokes were not of the merriest. I hated it. All I could do was endure and hope to survive. Was it for this I'd been through all that? Myrtle coming to lunch after I'd been there a year saying bluntly, 'Are you better?' brought a smile of relief to my face. 'You'd better ask them,' I replied. 'Oh much better,' they said fervently, 'We can tell jokes around you now.'

My tiny room and the crowded staffroom with no elbow room brought a return of claustrophobia. Work was a help. Children are always themselves. In the lunch hour I exercised and slept and renewed my energy for the afternoon.

It was now that anger came to the rescue.

At low points fantasies are correspondingly high. The end of all suffering and striving was not meant to be this: a job I didn't want to do, followed by a return home to spend the evening and the night alone. Friends having respected my need for solitude continued to do so. Coming home to my parents' house, my world ironically and cruelly had come full circle. Here were all my memories: of growing up, of

178

the war, of Mother's illness and death and then my father's. I would never get away from it. The time spent elsewhere, although that included twenty years of marriage, seemed negligible.

It was not fair. I couldn't afford to move. The time off work and Dr P's fees (which were always ridiculously low) had swallowed up the little money my father had left me. Hoist again, though not with quite the same petard. If I'd been able to continue working full time I would have had enough money – but not enough anything else, like energy or desire or sanity. Round and round like a squirrel in a cage, anger spinning through my mind, contemplating what seemed like another impasse.

I didn't have migraine so often or so violently now, but when I did it felt like an expression of this frustration, the hard rock against which my anger beat in vain. Trying one day to relax and enter into the pain, to find some relief from it, I saw an image against my closed eyelids: a hard grey rocky cavern with no entrance, and inside where no one could reach immeasurable and innumerable treasures piled high: jewellery, silver and gold, swathes of beautiful cloth – a pirate's treasure. But quite unattainable. Only dynamite could break through the rock, and that would probably destroy the treasure as well.

The nights were the worst. After dark the house settled on its haunches with thuds and groans and creaks, as the temperature fell and old walls and timber stretched and contracted. It settled round me like an old musty well-worn cloak. The owl hooted. Could it be the same one I remembered from childhood, sailing slowly on tawny wings across the garden, faintly outlined against the trees, a ghostly shape on the fence with only its eyes moving and glinting in the moonlight? I slept in the same bedroom now. It seemed that it and I were the only wakeful creatures. Round about house lights dimmed and went out one by one. I was alone with my memories, my loneliness, my anguish and my anger. I didn't know what to do with myself. What was the point?

I lay down on the bed, my legs straight out, hands crossed on my breast. All I needed to complete the picture of a deathbed, a pure white lily in my hand. Perhaps God (who?) would take me in the night. I fell asleep and dreamed that I was walking by a river through pleasant fields with my father and my brother. Suddenly a huge gust of wind came from nowhere just as we reached a bridge and I was wondering if we were going to cross it. It picked me up and whirled me helplessly away. I tried to call for help but no sound came from my lips. My father and brother continued walking and talking as if nothing had happened.

That dream recurred in different forms. Once I was watching Mother as she sewed and again I was whisked helplessly away and she didn't notice. Always the wind I was helpless against, however hard I struggled. In its final appearance I was lying in bed. The wind tried to drag me out of the window. This time I got angry and fought against it with all my might, and thought, there's a lot of power here, perhaps I can use it. And I levitated, rising a couple of feet above my bed. So strong was the impression and so real that when I woke I tried to put my hand between myself and the bed. I was very disappointed to find I was just tamely and stodgily lying there.

But in between the first and the last of these dreams a lot had happened. (I always fought the wind. I wonder what would have happened if I had ever given in and let it carry me. Where? I never found out. I always woke up first.)

It was then in desperation that I began talking to God. I needed someone to blame. I had always blamed myself. That was over. This was not my fault. My responsibility, but not my fault.

Suffering does not ennoble, is not a necessary part of growth, though it may be a fact and a factor in it. It also warps, sours and embitters. It is the surviving, being able to go through and out the other side that strengthens, helps one to face Kipling's 'twin imposters'.

I had survived. I could live in the world, compete on equal terms, earn my living. But I did not expect to be happy. Did not even want to be, suspecting the hidden fetters of loving relationships. And I was bitter. Surviving is not enough.

A blind Samson I in my rage against this God
who gave me life and would not show me how to live.

Who to blame? My parents? Not much satisfaction in beating up the old and feeble. Dr P? It was too monumental even for her to bear.

The stronger I got the more my anger swelled. It fuelled me – brought back colour to my cheeks, a spring to my step. But it also kept me restless and wakeful. In the long nights when I felt most alone, when those I might have turned to were presumably sleeping at last I turned on God: the author of it all. The God I'd been taught about at school had never made sense to me – the perfect, the all-loving. The Old Testament God of wrath, of vengeance, a jealous God was more credible. But a fallible God? Even a non-believer jibbed at that. Supposing I was wrong? When I was young I had an agreement with God, hedging my bets: 'If you do exist will you forgive me for not believing in you?' But it would be more difficult for me to forgive God for letting things be so bad in the world, for not feeding the hungry. My father wouldn't behave like that.

I had always thought that if I got to heaven and found God sitting there I would let him have it. But now I couldn't wait. It all poured out. Why did you create such a lousy world? What right have you to inflict punishment on people who never did you any harm? (I didn't believe in Original Sin and the Fall.) What have I ever done to you? I've tried quite hard, again and again. Where did it ever get me? You bloody God. One long stream of anguish and despair and howling rage. (Quietly of course, I had to remember the neighbours.)

When it was over there was silence. Exhausted and empty I waited. No thunderbolt, no lightning strike. At least I wasn't being punished. He made me no answer, no sign. Had I expected one? I think I was always looking for proof, one way or another.

But there was relief. As if I had faced the final authority unafraid, and survived. I was my own woman. I didn't care for God. He didn't care for me. Fine. That was more honest than a pretence of love. And at least he wasn't vindictive (this God I didn't believe in).

Talking to God became a nightly habit. The one person to whom I could say exactly what I liked without a qualm. Even more impervious to insult than Dr P. I had a few sharp words to say about people who boast (or whose followers do) that they can number the hairs on anyone's head and not miss one sparrow that falls. As if. Who would believe that? Or is he so busy counting he doesn't notice the people who are starving? He can't have it both ways.

It was strange talking to a God I didn't believe in and only wanted to berate. Perhaps it was myself I was talking to. I was the only audience. Intentionally or not the effect on me was profound. Locked inside my head, denied outlet, the mess of feeling, the outrage had festered. Let out, articulated and clarified it acquired a reality, a validity and truth it hadn't had before. Hearing my own words clearly I could not doubt them. I had always been angry but had never been able to express my anger or even own it. I had turned it on no one but myself. Whether God existed or not I had to create him in order to find a legitimate outlet for my anger. And a strong enough container.

At work all my energies were bent on two things: on proving I could hold down a job and was therefore 'normal', and when that was established on finding a way out. The first took one year, the second nearly four.

When I began remedial teaching the training was minimal. We learned by trial and experiment. The teachers I worked with now were trained and qualified in remedial teaching. My only advantage, and it was considerable, was in years of experience and the confidence that brings.

Attitudes in education were changing, not always for the better. Methods from industry were beginning to be applied: time-and-motion studies and the maximisation of resources. Children are not merchandise. More is not necessarily better. Quality of work is always important. But education committees tend to be impressed by numbers. I worked best with individual children. Following the new trends all the other teachers worked with groups. As I also would have to if I stayed. The writing was on the wall.

I wanted out. And I was hardly in! I was not happy. I had never wanted to teach. It had been the only profession open to girls when I was young – that is girls without money. I like children but not in large numbers, and I don't like the 'press gang' attitude prevalent in many schools. Small children are naturally interested and curious. What do we do to them to ensure that so many lose their enthusiasm and become bored and unwilling prisoners? I would rather work with volunteers.

But I was middle-aged, what else could I do that would bring in a comparable salary?

For the time being I kept my head down, worked in my own way and was sufficiently successful to be accepted by both colleagues and authority.

But it was very lonely. Cutting myself off from my old social circles had been necessary, and for a time involuntary. It was much more difficult to begin again. Where would I find these mythical people, these new friends, the new life that I wanted? I was afraid that I might become stuck in repetition, in a continual regurgitation of anger and complaint leading nowhere except back into myself.

It was at this point that I had one of my 'images'. (I call

them that because I don't know what else to call them. I reject the term hallucination because it implies that they have no reality, except as a by-product of madness or drugs.) This was a bizarre, colossal image, the kind of image that might make you think you were mad. I had fallen into a restless sleep from which I woke in terror. Hanging from the light fixture over my bed was the most enormous rat − at least three feet long. This had to be a figment of my imagination, a trick of the shadowy light. I switched on my bedside light expecting it to disappear. It was still there. It made no move towards me, simply holding on to the flex with its front paws, swaying slightly and regarding me fixedly. But I was afraid to move in case it attacked me. I edged slowly upwards until I was sitting with my back against the headboard. It looked at me quite expressionlessly, unblinking. I was rigid with panic.

In the end I shut my eyes and said aloud, 'Please go away.' After a long pause I opened them. It had gone.

But I sat upright for the rest of the night with the light on, afraid to go to sleep in case it should return.

Next day I was still nervous, but in the cool light of day able to see that this was a rat of some significance. It was some time before I could look at it at all objectively.

Why a rat, which I've always been afraid of to the point of phobia? Why such a huge rat? And more particularly why such an unaggressive rat? It had done nothing but hang there; only saying by its presence, look at me. I didn't know why, but I couldn't ignore it.

In a perfect world there would be no rats. In a perfect world there would be no rat-like people. What is it about this one small creature that makes not only me fear and despise and regard it with loathing? Usually I can forget it as it lives underground and out of sight. I pretend it doesn't exist. But this one wouldn't let me do that. Was that why it was so ridiculously large? So that I should not ignore it?

Finally, when I could let it, it was the rat that taught me about survival. Rats are survivors. They adapt to almost every change in their environment, including every new poison we try. We wage a constant war on them. But they are still here.

If all my images are aspects of me then, reluctantly, so is the rat. The 'Mirror, mirror on the wall' does not only reflect back pretty pictures. Devious, sly, cunning, living in and off filth – whatever it takes to survive. That is the rat. Is it also me?

Survival is not nice. Did I ever think it was? People have turned cannibal in order to survive. It is not the good (they get theirs in the next world), it is the strong who survive. That was a lesson learned in the concentration camps.

So what was it saying to me? Don't just sit there, do something? And finally it made me laugh. At myself, my self-importance, my tragedy queen. It was a very puffed-up rat. 'Anything you can do I can do bigger.'

Song of the Rat

Oh Rat of mine, oh Rat of me.
I sing your cunning sly tenacity.
You tell them Rat. You shout it aloud –
in your tiny squeak that no one has heard –
'The God that made you is the God that made me.'

Oh shock, oh horror, oh deary-dear me.

'Poisons and ratcatchers, buckets and whips,
I laugh at your traps and I gives you the slip.'

Oh filthy invincible verminous Rat.

'Wherever you are that's where I'm at.
You build up your houses, you build up your halls.
You build them so strong, you build them so tall.
You scrub them and clean them, put paint on the walls –
down in the basement I'm coming to call.
You can't get away, no you can't get away
wherever you go for I'm here to stay.

Like Castor and Pollux, like Janet and John
we're always together world-wide and lifelong.

When you want to decide why you do what you do
why it's little old me you always turn to.
You skin me, dissect me, inject me and shock,
you maze me and haze me – all timed by the clock.
But you can't get away from or alter a jot
all the things that you are that you wish you were not.

Rat in the cellar, Rat in the hall,
Oh Rat in the mirror now who's fairest of all?
Dirty and devious and horribly bold: all the names you
can call.
I don't mind how you scold.
When your ship treasure-laden comes home from the sea
just remember who's first on the dock – why it's me!'

Tension and frustration were forcing me to look for something else. But the only decisive move I had made in my
entire life was when I left Nick, and that was more like
running away than a considered walk-out. Career moves and
personal moves like marriage had been instigated by someone
else – Mother, Nick – and I had merely persuaded myself
to go along with them and called that my personal decision.
Little acts of rebellion spattered my virtuous path: choosing
a college furthest away from home when I had been accepted
by several much nearer, opting to take a degree which was
not necessary for elementary schoolteachers. But that was all
they were. Mother was sure I would do best with young
children. Nick was sure I would be happy with him. I was
sure they were right.
    'Could I do what you do?' I asked Dr P diffidently.
    'Yes, why not?' She added, 'When you've got through all
this,' sketching a vague gesture to embrace 'all this'. Gratify-
ing, but I was a long way from through.
    That became something to hang on to. If I had learned
anything from 'all this' it would be good to be able to make

use of it, other than in the most general way that I already did. And so finally against all the advice and gloomy prognostications of colleagues I took early retirement and embarked on a course of training in counselling.

V

Another ending. Another beginning. But not in the neat and orderly way that looking back makes it appear.

I was going along from day to day, keeping my head down as I have said, and letting each decision take me by surprise – the only way I could be sure they were mine. If I made them deliberately (apart from the one to go back to work) I was always afraid that I would be too much influenced by other people's wishes. I knew that I wanted something else, something new. Consciously and unconsciously I was searching. I joined a succession of groups of other searchers, some weird and funny, some charlatan, one or two like the Centre for Transpersonal Psychology where new horizons were discovered. I don't remember the exact chronology, but in the same year that I finished analysis I began looking at counselling courses.

To say 'I finished analysis' does nothing to convey the agony of the process. I set one day, let it pass, set another, let that one pass, and finally one that I did adhere to. All the time saying, I can't do this, I can't go. It had gone on so long it was a way of life, it was my life. How could I manage without her? How could I bear not to see her?

As it began and continued so it ends, with an image. Over the years the different images of the witch – malevolent and benevolent – had merged into one: Dr P. She was the receptor and the rejector, the life-giving and the life-taking, the loved and hated one, the one I had to escape from, the one I had to kill. The one I had to survive.

The final image is straight from *Hansel and Gretel*. The children having been released from their magical bondage, are standing in a circle. In the middle the witch, flowing skirts, pointed hat and broomstick. She kneels on the ground, her head bowed. Over her stands one of the children with an axe raised high in preparation for its descent. The children have danced around the witch cheering and laughing. Now they are silent. The witch says she is sorry. And there the image ends, axe still poised, children still silent. Is it enough if the witch says she is sorry? I don't know, but there appears to have been a stay of execution. Perhaps it is.

We set a six-month fail-safe date. But when it came to the last session it was much easier than I had imagined. I realised that I was saying goodbye to a particular part of my life, to a particular room that had become my second home, but not now or ever to her. She was in my heart and would always be there. Sitting in the autumn twilight of a late Friday afternoon, in the glow of the gas fire, hearing it hiss softly and listening to the fall and rise of our voices in the conversation that over the years has become so familiar and so easy. We would not be sitting here perhaps like this but the conversation would go on.

Part V

'Only where love and need are one
And the work is play for mortal stakes'

Robert Frost

i

When I began this story it was under a compulsion I didn't understand, wondering why I wanted or needed to write it at all. Many more dramatic and soul-searing accounts of analysis have been written. And it adds nothing to theory. I can't write about myself with detachment.

My purpose became apparent only as I wrote, and found myself pulling together all the different strands; making some sense of some of them; seeing more clearly now, and discovering more objectivity with the distance of time. Then I was like a cork tossed on a vast ocean. Now I am in calmer waters.

It was a terrible, strange, wondrous, awful, amazing experience. And one finally I wouldn't be without. Equally one I wouldn't ask for or want to go through again. It is the surviving and what I discovered, what happened on the journey that makes it worthwhile. I found a kind of love I had not experienced or expected. I found some compassion for myself and some humility. I found surprising riches, not gold or silver but more valuable (the treasure of my migraine cavern that had been so inaccessible): being able to live as a real person in the real world. For me the most amazing and satisfying of all eventualities – to live as if I have the right to. It may sound dull to those who are able to take that for granted; not to me. It doesn't mean, as I once thought, 'putting away childish things'. I had done that as I was bid, and found myself cut off from the realms of imagination and creativity.

This time I have brought the child with me. And it is her ability to enjoy life, her curiosity and unending involvement in it that give life its savour. Boredom that was once a constant and dreaded companion is now rare. The difference not so much in newly discovered talents; but where I used to be solely dependent on those around me to give life meaning I now have sufficient resources within me: I can survive the bad times and enjoy the good.

I don't know how I seem on the outside; inside I am very different. Perhaps not that I am such a different person, but that I like myself better and feel more in charge of my life. Whatever there is, whatever I am, is me and is real. As the Skin Horse* said: 'Once you are real you can't become unreal again. It lasts for always.'

I began by describing this as a story about an ordinary life. Ordinary in that it was like many others. Ordinary also in the way I experienced it: as dreary and monotonous with little sense of purpose or joy or wellbeing. Existence as it is for many who see drama and romance only in the lives of others: stories they tell to comfort themselves, stories of one day and maybe.

It felt wickedly self-indulgent to spend so much money just talking about myself, and was something I would never have dreamed of if I had not been so desperate, and even then if it had not been suggested to me. Like charitable handouts that are reserved for those who can prove extreme need, I thought psychotherapy was only for the severely disturbed, for the insane.

What has changed is not being ordinary or extra-ordinary but how I feel about it. Paradoxically the more conscious I am of my separate identity, of my uniqueness, the more I am aware and the less I mind that I am ordinary: that is, humanly fallible and inadequate like everyone else.

Dr P once said when I admitted that I wanted to be perfect, 'Do you think people would like you much if you were? They would find it as awful trying to live up to you as you did trying to live up to your mother.'

Questions remain. Some hurt remains. It lurks still beneath

* *The Velveteen Rabbit*

the surface, and when prodded flares into life, a wound that closes but does not entirely heal. The impulse to self-destruction is still there. A necessary ingredient of self-preservation is missing. Like someone recovering from a stroke I am constantly forced to relearn what I already know but keep forgetting: what everyone else seems to know. Or is everyone like me for ever learning and relearning how to live?

Questions. Why did it take so long? I was often asked. The only answer I could give then and now is: it took as long as it had to. For the first few years I lived in constant anxiety that she would send me away. Then when I realised that she wasn't going to other worries surfaced, other questions. Am I too dependent on her? Yes. Could I work things out for myself as others do? No. Will I still be seeing her (or her equivalent) when I'm ninety? Possibly.

I couldn't believe that my particular life was worth living. I could see that other lives were. (Though I thought some deluded themselves.) The only point was in trying to find a point. The alternative was death – which I had rejected as unfair to my children – but remained a comforting option if all else failed. Would it ever end? I doubted it.

It was rather like recovering from an illness. One day you are still an invalid shrinking from the robust energy of those around and from every breath of fresh air. The next inexplicably you are better; still weak and tiring easily but definitely on the side of the living once more. When precisely that day will come is impossible to predict. You only know when it arrives.

On countless days I sat opposite her and knew that she spoke the truth: about the kind of life I could have and about the people who loved me; and it was like an edifice made of dust that crumbles when you touch it, having no substance.

Because I cannot drink
there, where trees flower
and springs flow . . .
for there is nothing again . . .

The falling roses are reflected in the polished table top, the slatted blinds cast stripes across the floor. The comfortable, unpretentious room is held under a dead weight of silence while outside a car goes by. She shuts her eyes and turns inward. And I look at her from a great distance. And see that she too is nothing. Not in herself. But for me. I have destroyed her again. She is out of my reach, and I of hers.

She cannot possibly want me. She must hate me – despise me – if not she is only deceiving herself and one day she will. It might as well be now. She might as well admit the truth – that I am nothing – and my life is nothing. It is a litany of destruction and counter-destruction. 'Who have been cast out from Eden, allowed to enter at last must wreak havoc and destroy the very thing they have always longed for.' She can't win. Neither can I.

There came a day.

I can see her face: unfathomable. Is she angry? No, but serious, implacable, fixing me with a stern blue eye. I always know when she means business.

I don't remember what I had said to provoke this; the shock drove it from my memory. A threnody of my usual negatives, a catalogue of habitual nos and can'ts, I expect.

She sat squarely with her hands on her knees and looked at me. 'I have done everything I can. I can do no more. The rest is up to you. I can't make you believe me. If you do or not is up to you now.'

She had rendered me speechless. For it was true. She had done everything. Passed every test. Always been there: supporting me, occasionally failing me; understanding me, misunderstanding me; agreeing with me, arguing with me. Liking me, it often appeared, much better than I liked myself.

Steadfast. Holding my hand, refusing to go away however much I rejected her. Keeping what I would destroy. Loving me when I could not love myself.

She had done all that. And was not saying that she was going to stop. Simply that there was nothing else she could do. There was the water. Would this horse drink, or die of thirst? And I knew that also was true. That it was up to me.

She stirs, making the infinitesimal movements that signify the end of the session, and smiles as if to take some of the bleakness out of her statement.

I can't describe exactly what that did to me. Frightened me for sure. But not in a devastating way. Intrigued. Curious. What does that mean? Not knocked sideways as I would expect. Discovering strangely solid ground beneath my feet. It was as if she had handed something back to me, something that always really belonged to me, but that I could not handle without destroying it, that she had kept safe for me, from me, and now was handing back saying: 'Here, take it, it is yours. You look after it now.'

To write that makes me want to cry even now. It was such a truly liberating thing. Such a gesture of faith. (I don't know if that was what it was to her. She seemed to speak from a mixture of exasperation and determination.) And it was, I think, the beginning of the end, the beginning of my true independence. Of my realisation that this was my life and I could choose to live it or not. Perhaps, to be truthful, was already living it – just afraid to admit it to myself. She was giving me a shove, saying, 'Stand on your own feet. You can.' And I could.

A dream: I woke to find mice playing on the carpet at my feet quite unafraid. I am terrified of mice so I called the cat to come and deal with them. The next time I looked they were all, cat and mice, lolling amicably against the wall chatting and laughing. I was furious, so incensed that I seized a broom and swept them all out into the garden. That was a very invigorating dream and made me smile whenever I thought of it.

Questions. Why did I have to have everything so literally re-enacted? At the time I didn't question it. It was more a matter of responding to persistent demands from within, of trying to find a solution, of seeing what would work. I was never able to work anything out with my mother. I wanted something different from Dr Penny.

I am reluctant to answer the question myself. I don't feel qualified. But who should know me better? So far I have avoided the issue. But finally it has to be faced.

If analysis is a symbolic re-enactment of actual experience that cannot be literally repeated, what were we up to, Dr P and I? What comes to mind is, as always, an image. When my mother died I felt as if I was the surviving half of a pair of Siamese twins; a position I had not known myself to be in. The bond had been invisible. Only its severing announced its existence. I was forced to recognise it by the nature of the raw and bloody wound in my side.

The image is of myself curled foetus-like against my mother, and of a sharp axe descending, ripping us apart. I should not survive but I do, though the wound continues to bleed. The wound is irreparable. The best we can do is to pretend it never happened. Which is how my parents behaved; and so did I apparently. 'In no time at all you were your usual fat, smiling happy self,' my father said many years later. Mother used to say I was a ray of sunshine lighting up the room whenever I came in. I only remember coming into rooms hesitantly and with trepidation.

Only something that severe, that irrevocable can explain how I feel. We talk of splitting and the need for reintegration, the bringing together of opposites, the acceptance of ambivalence. This does not seem to belong in the same category. Here are two halves that cannot be brought together again. Perhaps because of the severity and the totality of the split.

Thinking of it now, it is like cutting off a gangrenous limb

196

to save the rest of the body. I had to be cast off because I contained all the bad things that the organism was better without. That is different from the way it is usually seen. I did not project the bad into the other but the good. Or was I really the projection of, the container for my mother's badness? To keep her alive and good, the badness, the wrongness had been put into me and discarded; and to keep her alive there it had to stay. That feels like the truth, that is, the truth as I saw it. Mother was always right, and unless I agreed with her I was always wrong; it was better that way, more comfortable. That explains why I felt that I was no good, though I tried to disguise it. 'Assume a virtue if you have it not,' seemed to be written for me. It was my goodness, my sense of value that I had lost, so thoroughly that I didn't believe in its existence. I experienced total rejection and it became a battle for survival. This battle was acted out in dreams in which my mother was always trying to kill me. In order to survive I had to kill her.

I was unable to take the breast or any kind of food. I have an image of myself lying in my cot smelly and dirty. Knowing my mother I can't believe that she would ever leave me so. In reality I expect that the discomfort and the pain were such that I could find no relief, and no comfort in being held.

This is how it felt: the cutting off from all life, all nourishment; a separation too abrupt, too complete, too severe to be tolerated; too early for separation to happen naturally. The attachment is simply not there, however much it may be simulated. How can a baby come to terms with a loss that has already happened, happened prematurely and so savagely before it was ready? How can it learn to tolerate separation from what already feels agonisingly separate?

Life does not begin for me when I was born. In my memory life begins with illness, with rejection, with death, and a slow crawl back to life against the odds.

I have tried to get in touch with that baby that was alive before the illness. But I cannot. I can take myself back through my life, pressing the rewind button until I reach the age of eight months. Beyond that nothing. I cannot envisage my birth. If I try to force it my mind jumps to a prebirth state, a limbo in which I am simply resisting being born. It is a very powerful taboo that will not allow me to acknowledge the baby that was born to, connected to and fed by my mother, and was by all accounts happy and contented. Although I know it was me even now I have to say that baby is not me. That baby died. All I can do is mourn her. Something was irrevocably lost, something that could never again be taken for granted. Something – like connection, bonding, intimacy, trust – that I was not able to live without. That's why it all had to be done again.

Here we come to the paradox. I talk of irrevocable loss, but begin by describing myself and my mother as Siamese twins; an invisible bond between us so strong that only death can sever it; a relationship I repeated in my marriage.

Both statements are true. It was a desperate union in which each needed the other to survive; as two halves of one whole, a union that had existed once, and I was always trying to recreate. But there is no real intimacy, only terrible loneliness and isolation beneath apparent harmony. Nothing can grow where there is no true wholeness. Having been disastrously wrenched apart they can only simulate, desperately clinging, what they have never known. One hears occasionally of limbs that have been cut off and sewn back on again. If my mother had been able to hold me close enough for long enough perhaps I might have grown together again. But she didn't know how to. Nor did she know it was necessary. That would have been the way to save my life. Not just by not letting me die. That was never enough.

But Dr P did know. She held me until I had had enough, until I was ready to be let go. She let me say when.

Developmentally an eight-month-old baby is beginning to

recognise its mother as a separate person with needs of
her own. It is the beginning of a physically separate and
independent life: crawling, standing, walking. By all accounts
I didn't crawl at all. I sat on my bottom until I was nearly
two and then suddenly stood up and walked. It sounds to
me like an early version of a sit-in. I guess I finally realised
I couldn't win. They weren't going to let me go back and
do it all again. Sooner or later I had to move.

ii

You spend your whole life trying to please and fit in. You
hope that others will be equally concerned to please you.
But it doesn't work like that. They probably don't realise
that you have any needs. So assiduous have you been in
attending to theirs that they think you like it that way. In
time you come to feel like one who is starving in a land of
plenty. No one notices your outstretched hand, your gaping
mouth.

The moment arrives when for the first time you are aware
of your own hunger, of the enormity of your wants and
your despair of them ever being fulfilled. Then you realise
that life isn't a soup queue for the deserving, and that indeed
the Lord does appear to help those who help themselves,
which was always a rather immoral sort of a joke to us.
In our family helping yourself came under the heading of
delinquent behaviour.

The change brought about in me by analysis was summed
up by Jessica: 'If there were four bananas, one for each of
us, I always knew that you would take the smallest one. Now
I'm not so sure.'

For the first time you want to stop looking after other
people and doing what they want, and begin to do what
you want: please yourself, give yourself things, the things

that you always expected would one day fall into your lap like ripe fruit – providing you'd been good enough. And oh, you'd been good – coming out of your ears with it, so good you'd been!

But how to reverse the habits of a lifetime, yours and theirs? Their expectations of you, parents and friends who know they can count on you and get very upset when you begin to put your own needs first, and may call you selfish. And yours of them: firstly, that if you work hard enough, are good enough and pleasing enough they will eventually give you what you want, which, like the constant hope of a donkey following a carrot or a greyhound chasing a hare, is an illusory but sustaining myth it is hard to relinquish: secondly, and conversely, that if you stop trying to please them they will reject you and you will be alone again.

There is only one way to find out. You have discovered that your first assumption was wrong because here you are still waiting and wanting, for all your hard work. But what happens if you begin to look after yourself and neglect them? It is then you discover that it is not an either or world. Sometimes it is neither nor, but sometimes and and. It is not a soup kitchen. There are no free gifts, other than those you were born with or your parents were able to provide. But neither is it entirely a jungle of murderous rivalry and competition. Some people will reject you when you begin to put your needs ahead of theirs; others will be glad for you. The people who matter to you most will not stop loving you and may even feel relieved that you can look after yourself. The riches of the world are there for you to enjoy as much as anyone. The only entrance fee is being born. The price, taking into consideration what you may already have paid in unnecessary suffering, may or may not be too high. But it can never be as bad as the one that you have always anticipated, because, good or bad, it is real and reality is always preferable to illusion.

iii

And now . . .

As so often seem to happen, just when everything appeared to be going smoothly, for a third time I nearly died. I say appeared to be: I had a new career, a new home and good friends old and new, and I was enjoying life. But inside me there was a niggle of doubt, a faint question mark, a feeling I couldn't explain that something was not right.

I had smoked since the days when it was considered sophisticated, when Paul Henreid's way of lighting Bette Davis's cigarette was copied by every boy in the cinema. I was an addict and not sufficiently in love with life to be swayed by any anti-smoking propaganda. So it is not surprising that I finally got lung cancer. What did surprise me was how angry I was. I had after all allowed it to happen. I had gambled and lost.

It was ironic. For years I had wanted to die. For more years the only thing that sustained me was a grim determination to make something of my life. If I had a prayer in my unbelieving heart then it was, don't let me die before I have lived. And now when I was at last living with enthusiasm I was going to die. I was very frightened. But most I was angry. I didn't want to die. I wanted to live.

With my eyes shut I was aware of hands lifting me gently, sitting me up. As I regained consciousness the pain tore through me, searing, burning, unbearable. I opened my eyes to a circle of smiling faces: my children, pale-faced and sweating, bleary-eyed, lovingly beaming; the nurses, more detached but very pleased; Mr Greengrass holding my hand, feeling my pulse, patting me, saying, 'There, you've done very well, that's fine, everything's fine. Doesn't really hurt much does it?' in the tone that some doctors adopt, as to an idiot child, when they've inflicted every kind of indignity on you and hope you're not going to be so awkward as to mention it. I clung desperately to his hand as if I thought that would stop it hurting. My lips moved but no sound emerged. Lottie bending down heard me say, 'You lying bugger. It does hurt.' They had brought me to without drugs or sedatives to check that my lungs were working again. Later I was sedated and the pain became manageable. But it was that pain that I remembered, and it was the best kind of aversion therapy whenever I wanted a cigarette.

Dr P came to see me and I held her hand and told her how frightened I was: once again suspended over a black emptiness, floating in a fog of sedation that held pain and fear at a distance but in its lack of substance gave added weight to the nightmarish quality of my drug-induced hallucinations. One night I was convinced that the doctors and nurses were having a party in the ICU. I didn't blame them, but I was a little surprised at their indiscretion and worried that they wouldn't hear me if I called.

> That this is a bad place I've come to
> I know by what it lacks.
> Now rain and bird–bespattered tables and chairs
> where once was food and wine, music and dance.
> In this clearing then among the rhododendrons
> surely couples whispered secretly of love.
> Now the grass grows high, long abandoned.
> What terrible deed has banished them all:
> sighs of nostalgia, echoes of laughter, scent of bouquets,
> and left this emptiness, this desolation?
> What outrage has voided the very air of love?

To this illness there was a different quality, however. This time as I recovered I was aware of hands; a sea of hands beneath me, holding me above the abyss, supporting me, sustaining me: loving hands. The last time I had such an image, I had fled from it as from the hounds of heaven. Now I could allow it, take comfort from it and let it contribute its healing benison to my recovery, let myself believe that I was loved.

I was lucky. They had found it in time. The cancer was completely removed.

Afterwards Lottie said, 'You know you nearly died. The doctor said it was touch and go.'

I was surprised. 'You should have asked me. I had no intention of dying.'

I was too full of life to leave it without an argument.

*

Yet again there has been a shift of mood.

I don't believe that there is a God who looks after each one of us personally. I rather think we are given the equipment and left to make what we can of it. Even if there were such a God I can't imagine why he or she would want to save my life rather than any other. But I do believe that one's attitude makes a difference and I did very much want to stay alive.

Although I don't believe in a personal God I do believe that I am part of something, something living and universal. I am whole and I am part, and if I am cut off from that of which I am a part I die. There is no Big Daddy, no judge, but there are laws: laws that govern all of life and living things, and if these laws are flouted we pay the penalty. I have experienced that myself in many ways. We are all experiencing it now with the environment – to our amazement.

That I wanted to live may have helped. But still I was lucky. It might have gone the other way. So this time – these years, months, days, hours, minutes – is a bonus; not in the original script. I haven't done anything to deserve it.

203

Continuing to smoke in the face of all the evidence is not very clever. But I'm still here.

Seeing clearly and incontrovertibly for the first time that there is not a causal connection between 'one's just deserts' and the rewards of life enables me to take, to grasp, to grab with both hands as never before – relatively speaking. And because I feel so rich there is a different quality to my giving. I'm not trying to improve my score on the heavenly merit board. I'm not trying to please anyone but myself. But suddenly there is enough and more to go round. I can give without being depleted. I am more confident of the value of what I have and less ready to squander it. When nothing mattered, least of all myself, I spent my energy heedlessly on anyone or anything, whatever was asked of me until I was drained and exhausted. I had nothing better to do. Now I have.

Envoi

And now I am no longer young. I am not even middle-aged. I am old. I don't feel old. My body has slowed down a lot. I can't dance all night or even for half an hour. But inside I am much as I always was, inside I feel young, always excited about something and ready to laugh or cry. If my body can't my spirit still dances. I do not recognise the face in the mirror. I know it's mine, I see it every day, others recognise it. But it looks old and wrinkled and worn, not how I feel. Even that's not always true. Sometimes I feel very old and worn. Nevertheless there is one big difference. Now, quite often and for a lot of the time in fact, I am happy.

The abyss is still there. There are depths and there are heights. I may and do still fall. I tried, indeed was taught to keep to the straight and narrow, to stay on an even plateau and avoid the dangers of the precipice and the mountain path. That was easy for me, I was timid; heights made me giddy. And if I fell, I knew I would fall for ever into eternal damnation. Even if it had been possible to live like that, had been as simple as my parents made it appear, how dull it would have been. How dull it was. I nearly died of that. For somewhere inside my timorous body lurked a more adventurous spirit, an unsatisfied explorer who wanted to live dangerously and experience everything.

In the event I didn't have that much choice. I was not in control of my life however much I tried to be. And in finding that out I discovered that it is possible to fall and rise again, to die and live again. Nothing is for ever.

Recently I was ill and all the old feelings returned: there was no solidity in the earth beneath me, only a yawning chasm; I would surely die. I had workmen in the house. They made me cups of tea and dispersed my feeling that nobody would care if I lived or died. I was able to acknowledge my need and accept their help. In the unlikely event of my dying from a mild attack of flu, at least it wouldn't be because nobody cared. So I go down, and I come up again.

When I am down it is difficult still to believe in any other state of mind. Even my intellect deserts me. I am in a dark place, and my life is nothing but a pathetic failure: the things I haven't done, or have attempted and failed, the books I haven't written and now never will, the places I have never been, the people I have never known, the perfect lover I have never found: the catalogue is endless. (At least I can now leave my physical imperfections off the list. They have ceased to bother me.) The pages of my life stretch monotonously before me into a future which I know will be no different from the past. That I have been here before and know I will come out of it is my only comfort.

The death I always feared, though I didn't know it, was death in life: abandonment and rejection, the death of love, which I had to experience as a reality before I could begin to live. Real death I can't anticipate.

The river runs beside me now. It is the source of life; it is life itself; it runs fast, it runs slow, it chasms down precipitous slopes, lingers in rocky pools, flows gently, stagnates, reaches finally the sea and loses itself there. Sometimes I am in it, sometimes on the verge looking on. When I die perhaps I shall cease to be separate and shall become wholly a part of it.

11 July 1988–20 September 1992